M.E. KERR

WHAT I KNOW
ABOUT
WRITING

HarperCollinsPublishers

9001295

ACKNOWLEDGMENTS

SHORT STORIES

"The Author": *Funny You Should Ask*, edited by David Gale, Delacorte Press, 1992
"The Green Killer": *Bad Behavior*, edited by Mary Higgins Clark, Harcourt Brace & Company, 1995. Reprinted by permission of the publisher
"I Will Not Think of Maine": *Family Secrets*, edited by Lisa Rowe Fraustino, Viking, 1998
"Like Father, Like Son": *Scholastic Scope*, November 1995
"Sunny Days and Sunny Nights": *Connections*, edited by Donald R. Gallo, Delacorte Press, 1989

NOVELS

Fell: Harper & Row, 1987
Gentlehands: Harper & Row, 1978
I Stay Near You: Harcourt Brace & Company, 1996
Little Little: Harper & Row, 1981

AUTOBIOGRAPHY

Me Me Me Me Me: Harper & Row, 1983

Library of Congress Cataloging-in-Publication Data
Kerr, M. E.
  Blood on the forehead : what I know about writing / M. E. Kerr.
    p.   cm.
  Summary: Using examples from five novels and five short stories, young adult writer M. E. Kerr offers insights into ways writers can get ideas and create successful stories.
  ISBN 0-06-446207-2 (pbk.). — ISBN 0-06-027996-6
  1. Kerr, M. E.—Authorship—Juvenile literature.   2. Fiction—Authorship—Juvenile literature.   [1. Kerr, M. E.—Authorship.   2. Fiction—Authorship.   3. Authorship.]
I. Title.
PS3561.E643Z464   1998   97-41953
808.3—dc21   CIP
                                                                           AC

1   2   3   4   5   6   7   8   9   10
❖
First Edition

THIS BOOK AND SO MANY
others could not have been written without the kind
and generous spirit of Beth Gray and her staff at the
East Hampton Library: Diana Dayton, Debbie Donohue,
Sheila Dunlop, Joyce Flohr, Kate Galecka, Dorothy T. King,
Jane Reutershan, Elizabeth Sarfati, Jeanne Voorhees,
Ola Walker, and John Walden.
And what would I have done without their very special
performances to cheer us all on holidays?
Thanks!

BOOKS BY M. E. KERR

Dinky Hocker Shoots Smack!
Best of the Best Books (YA) 1970–83 (ALA)
Best Children's Books of 1972, *School Library Journal*
ALA Notable Children's Books of 1972

If I Love You, Am I Trapped Forever?
Honor Book, *Book World* Children's Spring Festival, 1973
Outstanding Children's Books of 1973, *The New York Times*

The Son of Someone Famous
(AN URSULA NORDSTROM BOOK)
Best Children's Books of 1974, *School Library Journal*
"Best of the Best" Children's Books 1966–1978,
School Library Journal

Is That You, Miss Blue?
(AN URSULA NORDSTROM BOOK)
Outstanding Children's Books of 1975, *The New York Times*
ALA Notable Children's Books of 1975
Best Books for Young Adults, 1975 (ALA)

Love Is a Missing Person
(AN URSULA NORDSTROM BOOK)

I'll Love You When You're More Like Me
(AN URSULA NORDSTROM BOOK)
Best Children's Books of 1977, *School Library Journal*

Gentlehands
(AN URSULA NORDSTROM BOOK)
ALA Notable Children's Books of 1978
Best Books for Young Adults, 1978 (ALA)
Best Children's Books of 1978, *School Library Journal*
Winner, 1978 Christopher Award
Best Children's Books of 1978, *The New York Times*

Little Little
ALA Notable Children's Books of 1981
Best Books for Young Adults, 1981 (ALA)
Best Children's Books of 1981, *School Library Journal*
Winner, 1981 Golden Kite Award
Society of Children's Book Writers

What I Really Think of You
(A CHARLOTTE ZOLOTOW BOOK)
Best Children's Books of 1982, *School Library Journal*

Me Me Me Me Me: Not a Novel
(A CHARLOTTE ZOLOTOW BOOK)
Best Books for Young Adults, 1983 (ALA)

Him *She Loves?*
(A CHARLOTTE ZOLOTOW BOOK)

I Stay Near You
(A CHARLOTTE ZOLOTOW BOOK)
Best Books for Young Adults, 1985 (ALA)

Night Kites
Best Books for Young Adults, 1987 (ALA)
Recommended Books for Reluctant YA Readers, 1987 (ALA)

Fell
Best Books for Young Adults, 1987 (ALA)

Fell Back
Finalist, 1990 Edgar Allan Poe Award, Best Young Adult Mystery
(Mystery Writers of America)

Fell Down
ALA *Booklist* Books for Youth Editors' Choices, 1991

Linger
1994 Books for the Teen Age, New York Public Library

Deliver Us From Evie
Best Books for Young Adults, 1995 (ALA)
Recommended Books for Reluctant YA Readers, 1995 (ALA)
Best Books of 1994, *School Library Journal*
Fanfare 1995: *The Horn Book*'s Outstanding Books of the Year
Finalist, *The Hungry Mind Review*,
1995 Children's Books of Distinction
1995 Books for the Teen Age, New York Public Library

"Hello," I Lied

CONTENTS

AUTHOR'S NOTE

F I WERE TO LOOK UP FROM MY COMPUTER NOW, I would see a favorite quotation in a frame over my desk, attributed to Gene Fowler:

Writing is easy: all you do is sit staring at a blank sheet of paper until the drops of blood form on your forehead.

In *Blood on the Forehead* I share what I know about writing short stories and novels.

A short story gives you a glimpse of something, while a novel lets you have a good, long look. But whichever you choose to write, there are certain courtesies the writer should extend to the reader:

1. *Don't cheat the reader.* Don't write a story that leaves out an important fact that should have been mentioned at the very beginning—for example, that the main character is an elk. (Surprise, surprise!)

2. *Take the trouble to give your characters interesting names.* "Mary Smith" isn't a good choice.

3. *Don't tell a story in heavy dialect or slang.* Your reader shouldn't have to plow through it to "hear" you.

4. *Grab your reader right away.* " 'Where's Papa

going with that axe?' said Fern to her mother as they were setting the table for breakfast." . . . It sounds like the start of a Stephen King novel, but it's actually the beginning of a classic children's book, *Charlotte's Web*, by E. B. White.

5. Grace your work with a provocative or appropriate title. John Steinbeck claimed he wasn't a title man, that he didn't care what his book was called. A good thing, because when *The Grapes of Wrath* was published in Japan, it was translated as *The Angry Raisins*.

6. An idea is not a story. Focus on the conflict, and remember that you're not finished until you've given your reader at least a hint of how your character will change, or how the problem will be solved.

7. Be as direct as possible. It took me a long time to realize that it's easier for the reader if I put down events in the order they take place. Flashbacks stop the momentum, and often force the reader to go back and reread.

8. Don't expect the reader to stick with you if you veer away from the story. Every scene should advance the plot. Keep on track.

9. Show your reader; don't tell him. Don't just say a boy is a bully. Describe him as he belittles a defenseless victim. Write a mean scene.

10. *Cut! Cut! Cut!* Your reader has a life.

Easy reading is hard writing. Nobody sees the blood on the forehead, just the smile on your face after there's an A+ at the top of your composition, or your name is under the title of a published book. While everyone, at one time or another, is made to write something, few people are self-starters, and even fewer go on to become professional writers. I once had a creative writing teacher who told the class, "If there is any way you can keep yourself from being a writer, do it!" (This man had published several books. He wasn't just a writer. He earned his living teaching.)

I thought his pronouncement was cruel and arrogant. I was struggling to produce short stories for his class. I wrote and rewrote these stories, and half the time he returned them with his blunt comments scrawled across the bottom of the last page.

Things like:

Don't unload on me! I want a story, not a summary of your life!

I hear your characters but I don't see them!

Why do I have to wait five pages for you to get around to beginning your story?

Many years and many novels later, I finally understood what he was all about.

If you are a writer, you won't be *able* to keep yourself from being one.

You may have to drive a truck, wait tables, join the army, or teach, as this man did, but somewhere you will have a story started, lines of a song or a poem written down, a novel or one act of a play under way, and you'll keep working at it while you earn your living.

If you are a writer, you'll be tough enough to stay with it, no matter what.

Criticism goes with the territory. You will never like getting it, and you may never warm to the person giving it, but you'll learn from some of it . . . and some of it you'll learn to ignore.

Nine times out of ten, if you're a writer, your childhood made you strong in ways you didn't realize when you were young. You have things to be thankful for that you once believed would do you in: someone's cruelty, someone's death, someone's rejection, someone's inability to love you, or someone's prejudice.

One great thing about writing is that in a very gratifying way you're eventually paid back for all the bad things that ever happened to you. The worse they are, the more gold you have for your "golden tale."

When bad things happen to good people, good

writers become alchemists. If you don't know what that word means, look it up. If you're going to be a writer, someday you'll remember finding that word in the dictionary . . . and finding, along with it, a name for the magic inside you that will eventually turn things around.

Because of it, losers become winners. Nerds and dorks become heroes.

I am a lover of rock music, and I live in a community where many rock stars live or visit. Some of them I have interviewed. Hands down, all of them tell me their teenage years were miserable. They weren't popular or they weren't good students. They were ugly or they were poor. They were shy or they were bullied. Most of them are yesterday's losers.

Today they write the songs.

This book is dedicated to the kids who hope someday to write the songs, whether they're novels, poems, plays, essays, or the kind of songs you sing. It's also dedicated to their teachers, very often the first ones to recognize their talents and to cheer them on.

M. E. Kerr

❦ SHORT ❧ STORIES

THE DIFFERENCE BETWEEN A SHORT STORY AND A novel is the difference between a visit to a nearby town and a trip to another country.

To visit the nearby town you don't pack much, you don't have as far to go, fewer people are involved, and you take a direct route to your destination.

You don't ramble, or sightsee as much, either, and because your time is limited, your intentions are clearer. In a short story, something happens and the writer narrows in on that. In a novel, many things happen and the focus is broader.

I lead a writing workshop, and members of the class sometimes bring in short stories from magazines like *The New Yorker*, famous for launching the careers of many writers such as J. D. Salinger, who wrote the novel *The Catcher in the Rye*.

These magazines often publish a kind of story called "a slice of life."

"Nothing happens!" my writers complain. "Isn't

a short story supposed to have a beginning, a middle, and an end?"

Many of these shorts aren't structured. Sometimes they're chapters from writers' novels-in-progress, and other times they're little more than brief views of a few people in situations that have no clear outcome. You finish reading a story like that, and you're not sure what the author meant to tell you.

Often the author isn't telling you anything in particular, merely giving you a snapshot study of characters caught in an interlude, leaving you to ponder how that interlude affects them.

The writing in this kind of short story can be very powerful and provocative, but few amateur writers are skilled enough to succeed at it.

The beginning writer is better off sticking to the traditional short story before trying to write a "slice of life," just as the beginning artist usually has to master drawing from models and still lifes before venturing into abstract painting.

Often when a writer in our workshop reads a story he or she is developing, someone will ask, "What's at stake here?"

The writer should be able to answer that question: state what the problem is, what change is in the wind, what's happening that's significant enough to grab the reader's attention. Novels have plots and many different voices. Short stories have themes (bravery, rejection, jealousy, etc.) and only one or two viewpoints. Always there is a change brought about, for better or worse, and the tension in the story comes from watching it come into being.

Now I think primarily as a novelist, but when I was younger, I honed my craft writing short stories for the many magazines there used to be that regularly published fiction.

When I was in boarding school, and then college, I used to set aside time once a week to work on a short story, for no other reason than that I loved writing one.

Now, as a professional writer, I have to worry about earning my living. The diminishing market for the short story doesn't encourage me to take time out, very often, to try one. (Most of the short stories in this book came about because an editor asked me if I would like to contribute a story to some anthology.) It isn't just the money, either. It's the thought that after you finish a story, it may never be published. One of my workshop writers calls his mailbox Heartbreak Hotel, because his short stories are so often waiting there for him, in the self-addressed envelope, with the rejection letter attached. He would gladly forgo payment just to see some of them in print.

I miss writing shorts. You don't have time to get bored with your characters. You don't have to check back to be sure of their hair and eye color. The seasons outside your window don't change. You don't either. It's a sweet, short visit, and you're never far from home.

❧ 1 ❧

Sitting Next to an Idea

"Sunny Days and Sunny Nights"

Unlike an idea for a novel, an idea for a short story often comes about by chance.

The idea for "Sunny Days and Sunny Nights" sat down next to me on a small plane taking me from Charlotte, North Carolina, to Greenville. (I am not a happy flyer, and I try to avoid the kind of little airplane where the "flight attendant" welcoming you aboard is not aboard herself, but is a voice on a tape.) The weather that day was freezing rain, and some of the salesmen—regulars on this route—were making jokes about a sudden loud noise as we speeded down the runway.

"There goes the wing" kind of jokes, and "No, that wasn't the wing, it was the motor." I was terrified.

Suddenly the young sailor who was my seatmate sighed and said, "I don't know which would be worse: not getting to Greenville or getting to Greenville."

I hadn't really looked at him until he said that.

He was very young, and his peaches-and-cream complexion, pug nose, and curly blond hair lent him an innocent look. He had a real Southern accent and a wide white smile.

"What's so bad about getting to Greenville?" I asked him.

"My girlfriend's father will be waiting at the airport," he said. "I just met him once, and afterward he told her I was a lia-, liabil-, a . . ." He fumbled for the word.

"Liability?"

"Right. A risk. He's a lawyer. I was a surfer back then, and he told her I'd never have a profession, that I was headed nowhere."

I forgot about the storm, and the "flight attendant" who was safely back on the ground somewhere, as Larry continued his story.

Next to his girlfriend, surfing was his great love. But he'd joined the Navy so he could get an

16

education, and now, thanks to the Navy, he also had a profession.

"What is that?"

"I'm an underwater welder!" he said proudly. "I'm one of the best, too! But I don't know if someone who's a lawyer is going to accept that. He told his daughter he bet I'd never have an office she could visit and then go off to lunch somewhere with me. He said the closest she'd ever come to anything like that would be to bring me a sandwich down to some worksite where I'd be this hard-hat laborer."

Larry pulled a picture of his girlfriend out of his wallet and told me he was going to propose to her, no matter what kind of welcome her "old man" gave him this trip.

Then, before I knew it, we were making a very bumpy landing, and Larry was peering out the small cabin window, seeing if he could see her . . . and her father.

Larry helped me with my baggage, and we ran through the rain into the small terminal.

There were a few people waiting to greet our flight, one carrying an M. E. Kerr book. She was the teacher assigned to meet me for a school visit.

Larry was looking around expectantly, but no one came forth to greet him.

He looked worried.

I couldn't keep the teacher waiting, so I said, "Good luck, Larry," and he said, "Thanks. . . . I wonder if they got my flight time right."

I left him standing there. I looked back once or twice, but the last time I saw him, he was still alone, with a large navy-blue duffel bag at his feet.

Of course, I never knew what happened . . . but for the rest of that weekend I thought about him, and he stayed on my mind for over a year.

Finally I wrote "Sunny Days and Sunny Nights," the story he inspired.

One of the best things about short story writing is that you only have to give the reader a glimpse of life, just as sometimes you only get a glimpse of someone you'll never forget, and never see again.

⊰ Sunny Days ⊱
and Sunny Nights

"Females prefer chunky peanut butter over smooth, forty-three percent to thirty-nine percent," Alan announces at dinner, "while men show an equal liking for both."

My father likes this conversation. I think even my mother does, since she is telling Alan enthusiastically that she likes smooth. Moments before she confided that she preferred red wine, after Alan said that women are more likely than men to order wine in a restaurant, and a majority prefer white.

Alan is filled with this sort of information.

He wants to become an advertising man. He is enrolled in journalism school for that purpose.

He's my height, when I'm wearing heels, has brown hair and brown eyes, lives not far away in Salisbury, North Carolina. We go out mostly to hit movies, and he explains their appeal afterward, over coffee at a campus hangout. He prides himself on knowing what sells, and why, and what motivates people. Sometimes when we kiss, I imagine he knows exactly what percentage of females close their eyes, and if more males keep theirs open.

I long for Sunny.

Whenever Sunny came to dinner, my father winced at his surfers' talk and asked him pointedly if he had a "real" name. Harold, Sunny would tell him, and my father would say, that's not such a bad name, you can make Harry out of that, and once he came right out and told Sunny that a man shouldn't have a boy's name.

When Sunny finally joined the Navy my father said, well, they'll make a man out of him.

He's a man, I said, believe me. Look at him and tell me he's not a man. Because Sunny towers over my father, has a Rambo build, and a walk, smile, and way about him that oozes confidence. Hair the color of the sun, deep blue eyes. Always tanned, always. Even my mother murmured, oh, he's a man, Sunny is.

But my father shook his head and said, I don't mean *that*. I mean the boy has a boy's ambition, you only have to listen to all that talk about the big waves, the surf, the beach—either he's a boy or a fish, but he's not someone with his eye on the future. He's not someone thinking about a profession!

One of the hard things about going to college in your hometown is that your family meets your dates right away. If I had the good luck to live in a dorm, my father couldn't cross-examine all of them while I finish dressing and get myself downstairs. Even when I'm ready ahead of time, he manages to squeeze out as much information about them as he can, once he's shaken hands with one, and while we're standing there looking for our exit line.

He likes Alan right away.

After dinner is over, while Alan and I go for a walk, Alan says, "I really like your family. Did they like me do you think?"

"I know they did."

But my mother never once threw her head back and laughed, the way she used to when Sunny was at the table, never said, oh, *you!* to Alan, like someone trying hard not to love his teasing—no one ever teased her but Sunny.

He'd tell her she looked like Princess Di (maybe . . . a little) and he'd often exclaim, you've made my day, darlin'! when he'd taste her special fried chicken. My father calls her Kate or Mama, and he can't eat anything fried because of the cholesterol, but they've been rocking together on our front porch through twenty years of marriage, and he *does* have a profession: law. He's a judge.

Oh, is he a judge!

Sunny, he said once when Sunny alluded to a future with me, every Friday noon Marybeth's mother comes down to my office and we go out to lunch. It's a ritual with us: I get to show her off to my colleagues, and we stroll over to the hotel, enjoy an old-fashioned, have the special-of-the-day, and set aside that time just for us. . . . I hope someday my daughter will be going down to her own husband's place of business to do the exact same thing.

Later Sunny said, He wasn't kidding, was he?

Him? I said. Kid? I said.

It was a week to the day that Sunny asked me to marry him. We were just graduated from high school. I was already planning my courses at the university when Sunny got wind of a job in Santa Monica, running a shop called Sun & Surf. Sunny'd moved from California when his folks broke up. His mom brought him back to Greenville, where she waited table in his grandfather's diner. . . . I never knew what Sunny's father did for a living, but my father, who spent a lot of time trying to worm it out of Sunny, said it sounded as though he was a "common laborer." Can't he be just a laborer? I said. Does he have to be a common one?

Marybeth, said my father, I'm just looking out for you. I like the boy. He's a nice boy. But we're talking here about the whole picture. . . . Does Sunny ever mention college?

I want to go to college, I told Sunny.

You can go out on the coast somewhere.

How? Daddy won't pay for it if we get married.

We'll figure out something.

It's too vague, Sunny, and too soon.

What's vague about it?

Don't *you* want to go to college, Sunny? Don't *you* want a profession?

Sunny said he couldn't believe I felt the way my father did, in the letter he left with my mother for me. He said the Navy was his best bet, and at least he'd be on water. He didn't say anything about waiting for him, or writing—nothing about the future. I'd said some other things that last night together, after he'd made fun of my father's talk about my parents' Friday-noon ritual. They don't even touch, he'd said: I've never once seen them touch, or heard them use affectionate names, or laugh together. So she shows up at his office once a week—big deal! . . . Honey, we've got a love that'd like to bust through the roof! You don't want to just settle for something like they did! They settled!

They love each other, I argued back, it just doesn't show. . . . Sunny said that was like plastic over wood, and love should splinter, crack, and burn!

You know how it is when someone criticizes your family, even when you might have thought and said the same things. You strike out when you hear it from another mouth, say things you don't mean, or you do, and wouldn't have said under any other circumstances.

I said, at least my father could always take care of my mother! At least he'd made something of himself, and she could be proud of him! That's good enough for me, I said. I knew from the hurt look in Sunny's eyes he was hearing that he wasn't.

"Seventy-four percent of American adults are interested in professional football," Alan says as we walk along under the stars. "Eighty-seven percent of men and sixty-three percent of women."

I can hear Sunny's voice saying blah blah blah blah blah blah!

"Alan," I say, "what kind of office does an advertising man have?"

"Mine's going to be in New York City, and there'll be a thick rug on the floor, and a view of the whole Manhattan skyline from the windows.

Do you like New York, Marybeth?"

"Anyplace but here!" I answer. "I'd like to get out of the South! I'd like to live near an ocean." I was picturing Sunny coming in on a big wave out in California. "I'd like to always be tanned."

Alan shakes his head. "That's out of style now. The ozone layer and all. No one wants a tan anymore."

When we get to the curb, Alan puts his hand under my arm and remarks, "You smell good. What perfume is that?"

"I don't remember what I put on." I was thinking of nights with Sunny we'd walk down this street with our arms wrapped around each other, and Sunny'd say, let's name our kids. Say we have four, two girls and two boys. You get to name a boy and a girl.

Alan lets go of my arm when we get across the street.

"I like the fact you're majoring in economics," he says. "You could go into investment banking. New York is where *you* want to go too."

"Sure, New York," I say. "That's for me."

Next weekend I have a date with John. Premed. Chunky. Beautiful smile. On the porch he tells my father, "I'll take good care of her. Don't worry."

"What are you going to specialize in?" My father gets one last question in as we are heading down the steps.

"Pediatrics, sir," and John grins and grabs my hand as we walk to his white Pontiac.

My mother is sitting in the wicker rocker on the porch, waving at us as we take off.

"Nice people," John says.

We drive to the SAE house with the top down, the moon just rising. "Your family reminds me of mine," he says. "Your mom so warm and welcoming, and your dad all concerned about me. . . . My father's that way about my kid sister when boys come to take her out. I don't have a lot of time to date, so I like dating someone whose family I can meet. You can tell a lot about a girl by her folks."

"They never touch," I tell him. "I mean, not openly."

"Like mine. You watch mine and you wonder how two kids got born."

We look at each other and laugh.

I like him. His wit, his good manners, his dancing, even his "shop talk" about his premed courses. He is a good listener, too, questioning me about what I'm studying, my ideas; he is the perfect date.

"Did you have a good time, sweetheart?" my mother asks.

"So-so." I tell the truth.

"In that case I hate to tell you what's on the hall table."

It's an overnight letter from Western Union. Short and sweet.

ARRIVING TOMORROW NIGHT. HAVE PROFESSION AND HIGH HOPES. LOVE, HAROLD.

"He's coming back, isn't he?" Mom says.

I show it to her.

"You like him, Mom, so why did you hate to tell me about this?"

"I like him a lot, but I don't think your father's ever going to resign himself to Sunny, even if he does call himself Harold."

"He has a profession, he says!" I am dancing around the room, hugging the letter. "He has high hopes!"

"I think he's the same old Sunny, honey, and I think it's just going to be more heartbreak. Oh, I do like him. Truly I do. But you started seeing Alan and John. You took a step away from Sunny."

"Just give him a chance, Mom."

"Give who a chance?" my father's voice.

He is coming into the living room in his robe and pajamas.

"Harold!" I exclaim. "Just give Harold a chance!"

"We used to chant 'Give peace a chance,' when I was in college," my father says, "and I'd say Sunny having a chance is like peace having a chance. Peace being what it is, and Sunny being what he is, no chance will do much to change things. Won't last. . . . Now, John is a young man I really warm to. Did you have a good time with John?"

"He was the perfect date," I answer.

"You said it was a so-so time," says my mother.

"Maybe I'm not into perfection."

When I meet the little plane that flies from Charlotte to Greenville, I can see Sunny getting off first, lugging his duffel bag, dressed in his Navy uniform, hurrying through the rain, tan as anything, tall, and grinning even before he can spot me in the small crowd.

He has a box of candy—"Not for you, my love," he says, "it's for your mama." Then he kisses me, hugs me, hangs on hard and whispers, "Let's name our kids. Say we've got six, all boys, first one's Harold junior. We could call him Harry."

There is no way I can get him to talk about his profession on the way home in my father's Buick. He says he is going to tell me at the same time he tells my folks, that all we are going to talk about on the way there is how soon I can transfer to the university near the base. He has three more years in the Navy and an application for reduced tuition for Navy wives, providing I still love him the way he loves me, do I? . . . *Yes?* Okay!

He says, "Park the car somewhere fast before we go straight home, because we've got to get the fire burning lower, or we'll scorch your loved ones. Here's a place."

My father growls, "One *hour* getting back here from the airport, was the traffic *that* bad on a weeknight? We thought you'd had an accident. . . ." And my mother purrs, "Guess what's cooking?"

"Fried chicken!" Harold cries, sounding like the same old Sunny. "Darlin', you have made my day! Love you and want some huggin' from my one and only!"

"Oh, *you!*" my mother says.

It does not take my father long to start in; he starts in at the same time he picks up his fork.

"What's this about a profession, Sunny? Harold?"

"Yes, sir, I am a professional man now."

"You're becoming a professional sailor, is that it?"

"No. sir. I'm leaving the Navy eventually, but thanks to the Navy, I now have a profession that suits me."

"Which is?"

"I'm an underwater welder."

"Let's eat before we get into all this," says my mother, fast.

"You're a *what?*"

"An underwater welder."

My father begins to sputter about Alan, who is going into advertising, and John, the aspiring baby doctor, those are professions, but what kind of . . . what kind of . . .

And my mother is passing the gravy, passing the cranberry relish, the biscuits, keeping her hands flying between the table and Sunny.

"Where will you, where will . . ." My father again, and if he ever finishes the sentence, I don't know. For I am seeing Sunny see me. I am seeing him be true to me and to himself. Perhaps my father wants to ask where will you do this, where will your office be, for my father is one to think in terms of a man's workplace.

But I am drifting in my thoughts to future Fridays, traditional and loving, donning a wetsuit for a rendezvous in the deep blue sea. Keeping my date with that warm fish I married.

❄ 2 ❄

Have You Ever
Been a Chicken?

"Like Father, Like Son"

I had an uncle who loved to tell jokes, and didn't
seem to know a single one that didn't manage to
offend *someone*.

He'd stand around at social gatherings rocking
on his heels, rattling the ice in his highball, and
asking people if they'd heard the one about:

The fat man.

The black man.

The Jew.

The priest.

The Puerto Rican.

The Italian.

On and on.

The one thing about him that amazed me was that no one ever walked away in disgust, punched him out, or crossed him off the next party list.

Most of his listeners laughed at his jokes.

He used accents, postures, hand gestures, and he had perfect timing.

"Joe doesn't *mean* anything," my mother'd defend him. "He's just having fun. . . . Why, Joe is one of the nicest men you'd ever meet anywhere. He wouldn't hurt a fly!"

My father, a small-town businessman, *did* object to his brother's jokes, but for the wrong reason.

My father'd say, "It's not right. We're in business in this town, and he could offend a customer."

Nowadays we're used to seeing sports coaches, politicians, corporate heads, ministers, writers, and so forth standing in front of microphones apologizing for things they said they claim they didn't mean.

Television talk show hosts have cut way back on ethnic jokes, sexist jokes, and jokes about sexual orientation.

The phrase "politically correct" is in all of our vocabularies.

But we all know that in our living rooms and

school yards, on the playing field, and at our parties, we haven't completely cleaned up our acts. . . . Maybe *we* don't tell the joke or use the offensive slang, but how many of us have the courage to get on the case of those who do?

I've been in situations myself where I held my tongue because I didn't want to make a scene, spoil a dinner party, or cause trouble among people I didn't know well.

I have a friend who sometimes chickens out in the same way I do. He'll nudge me and make a small clucking sound.

I wonder how many of us are "chicken" sometimes.

"Like Father, Like Son" addresses the "chicken" in those of us who are kept awake some nights, not by things we said but by things we didn't say.

⸎ Like Father, ⸎ Like Son

"Maybe you'd like us to call you something else," my father said to Harley.

"Why?" Harley said. "Just because it was a Harley my folks were riding when they were killed?"

"I know your real name's Ken Jr. I just thought—"

Harley waved away the suggestion. "I'm used to my nickname," he told my dad. "Anyway, it wasn't the Harley that killed them. They'd been celebrating their anniversary at Jungle Pete's, and Pop probably couldn't even see the road."

"OK. Harley it is!"

And Harley it was. In my room, while I slept on the sunporch hide-a-bed. Riding my 10-speed bike. Wearing my socks, my jackets. Playing my CDs, and hogging my PC. Harley made himself right at home.

"That's what we want him to do," my father said. "It won't be for long, Connor. His uncle's going to take him as soon as he finishes his work in Alaska. If it wasn't for Harley's dad, I wouldn't be alive."

Dad wasn't that surprised when he saw the swastika Harley had pinned to his cap the day we met his bus.

All Dad said was, "Better take that off, Harley. That won't go over too well here in Cortland."

"It's just a decoration—doesn't mean anything," said Harley, but he unfastened it and stuck it in his pocket.

The reason Dad wasn't surprised was that he'd been through the Gulf War with Harley's father, and he said Ken Sr. was a little "insensitive" too.

That was putting it mildly. After the war, he'd call Dad long distance and he'd always start off the conversation with the kind of jokes Dad hated: Polish jokes, jokes about Jews, blacks, Italians—no race or color was excluded.

If I ever told a joke like that, I'd be grounded, and Dad didn't have any buddies who spoke that way either. But Ken McFarland always got away with it.

"That's just Ken," Dad said. "He doesn't know any better. But he knew how to pull me out of the back of that Bradley when we got hit. He risked his life doing it, too!"

Both Dad and McFarland were reservists who suddenly found themselves in Iraq back when Saddam marched into Kuwait. . . . I was still in middle school then, wearing a yellow ribbon and an American flag, running to the mailbox every day, and never missing a Sunday in church.

I didn't dislike Harley. He was friendly and so polite my mother kept commenting on his good manners. We all felt real bad about his folks' death too, and we couldn't do enough for him.

But there were times, a lot of times, when my mother'd tell him at the dinner table, "We don't call people that, Harley." Or, "Harley? We don't think so much about a person's race or color."

He'd say, "Sorry, M'am. I don't have anything against anyone. I'm just kidding around."

"But I have a problem with it, Harley," Mom would try, "and it sounds like you *are* prejudiced when you talk that way."

"Not me," Harley'd tell her, always with this big smile he has, his blue eyes twinkling.

"Cork it around here!" Dad would say.

"Yes, sir. Right. I'll watch it," would come the answer. But there seemed to be no way he could stop himself. It was built-in. . . . Sometimes after my folks called him on it, they would roll their eyes to the ceiling, ready to give up on trying to change him. . . . I made up my mind I wasn't going to lose any sleep over it. He'd be gone soon.

He was a fish out of water in Cortland. He'd come in summer. I had a job waiting tables at Tumble Inn. Mom and Dad worked too, so Harley was home by himself a lot watching TV, playing computer games, riding my bike around.

He was fifteen, as I was, and he didn't have a lot of money, but Dad said let him have the summer off: Poor guy. Let him do what he wanted. He was going through enough.

He never showed that he was going through anything. He put a photograph of his parents out on my bureau, and he ran up our phone bills calling his buddies. He'd tell them eventually he was going to live with his uncle in Wisconsin. ("Yeah, I *know* it sucks!") And he'd ask a lot of questions about what was going on. Then he'd tell jokes like his father'd told—we'd hear him in my room hooting and howling, spewing the same kind of language my folks had called him on.

His uncle's job in Alaska took longer than we'd thought, and I dreaded it when I heard he was going to school with me come September.

Dad said he'd find his own crowd—let him be, so I let him be. I told kids I hung out with how his father had saved my dad's life, and what happened to his folks, and then I let him fend for himself.

Harley was really smart, and that surprised me. But he wasn't good at making friends. It was hard to be a new guy, too. We all knew each other since grade school.

Teachers warned Harley about his racist language. He always seemed surprised, and always protested that he was just kidding around. He *was* funny when he told his kind of jokes. The kids laughed at the accents he'd come up with, but he made them feel uncomfortable, too. . . . I'd just walk away, embarrassed for him, I guess . . . and embarrassed he was staying with us.

I'd see him sitting by himself in the cafeteria, looking around at everyone in groups. Once I felt sorry for him, and went over to sit with him. But he said, "You better get back to your crowd." I didn't ask him to join us. I knew he'd say something that would either trigger a fight or hurt someone's feelings. My father called him a "loose cannon," and I think that was why we didn't invite the neighbors over for our usual backyard barbecues.

He was a little guy: short for his age and he said he wasn't into sports. He didn't take to the rough-neck wiseguys he might have got along with better, if he'd made any effort. They ignored him, too.

I'd stayed on at Tumble Inn, after school started, working afternoons setting up tables, and weekend nights I was in the dining room. Harley was by himself a lot.

Don't ask me why Jitz Rossi got it into his head to go after him, but he did. It happened on a Saturday morning when Harley and I were walking back from town after helping Mom load the gro-ceries into her Pinto. She had other errands—it was a great fall day—and we decided to head back home along Highland Avenue.

Jitz was waiting for us at the top of the hill. He had his own Harley, and he was sitting on it, with a red-and-white bandanna around his forehead, a leather vest, and bikers' gloves. . . . A few of his buddies were behind him on their bikes.

The funny thing was Jitz wasn't that different from Harley. He was a lot bigger (star of the wrestling team), but he had the same "insensitiv-ity," as my father'd put it. He was a bully, though, and I think what got him going was that he figured

Harley's style was too much like his.

There was that nickname, too. That might have caught Jitz's attention.

The first thing Jitz said was, "How come you call yourself Harley?"

"It's my name."

"Where's your Harley?"

"I don't got one!" Harley laughed. "Got the name without the game."

"I hear you got a name for Italians, too," Jitz said. "I hear you're an outsider with a smart mouth."

Harley said, "I hear it only takes two people to bury your relatives, because there's only two handles on a garbage can."

What I remember after that little crack was Jitz getting off his Harley in perfect sync with the guys behind him. It looked like some kind of orchestrated ballet.

Next, this big bruiser had me down on the ground, slamming my head against the dirt.

What I didn't know was that Harley was a karate expert, and that there was more power in his small frame and tiny hands than there was in all four of the bikers who went after us. He took them on one by one, starting with Jitz, and then the guy holding me down.

After they all hobbled back on their bikes and

roared off, Harley brushed the grass and dirt off me and grinned.

My head and back felt wrecked and I had a nosebleed.

"Where would you dumb Micks be without the McFarlands to pull you out of tanks and up off your butts?" he said.

He was laughing and slapping his knee, and he didn't see my punch coming.

His body jerked back and one hand grabbed his jaw, and he looked at me wide-eyed. "What the HECK?" he said. "What's *that* for? I just saved your butt, Connor!"

"*That*," I shouted back at him, "is for making it necessary to save my butt!"

"You mad because I called you a dumb Mick?"

"I'm mad because we've been tiptoeing around trying to tell you you're this stupid toilet mouth! We hate the things you say! My dad hated your dad's dumb jokes. Every time he called my dad wanted to plug his ears!"

"My old man saved your dad's life!"

"Are we supposed to pay for that forever? When we go home, *you* get the hide-a-bed! Stop wearing my jacket. Put your dumb swastika back on and stay clear of me!"

I was starting down the hill, and Harley was

following after me. "Why didn't you say something?"

"We *did* say something!"

"Your mom and dad did. You never did!"

"I was trying to be nice because your folks died!"

"But *you* know I just kid around, Connor."

"From now on kid around somewhere else! I don't need my head banged in the dirt because you're this bigot!"

"You should have said something before."

"I'm saying it now! Get it? You're an embarrassment! You don't have a brain in your thick head!"

"An *embarrassment?*" He sounded really amazed. "I embarrass you?" He was trailing behind me, his voice suddenly a few registers higher than usual.

"That's right, and my family, too. You sound ignorant."

"I'm smarter than you. My grades are higher than yours."

That was true. He always made all A's. I said, "Yeah, but we can't take you anyplace with that mouth of yours. You're not fit. You sound like you crawled out of some gutter."

I don't know what else I said. I guess I said a lot of petty stuff, too, about him wearing my socks and using my PC too much. I just kept babbling away because of the pain I felt. I was finally tired of holding everything in, walking around on eggshells so as not to offend The Great Filth Mouth.

When I got home from work that night, he was in bed on the sleeping porch. His parents' photograph was out there with him on the wicker table near the alarm clock.

I told Dad what happened and he said, "I'm not surprised. Ken knew karate too. . . . But Harley's right. You should have said something before this. We owe that to friends, if we want to keep them for friends. *I* should have told Ken, instead of dreading our phone talks. We could have become real friends, but I missed that chance because I was too chicken to just say knock it off. . . . Now that you've cooled down, maybe you have more to say to Harley."

The next day my folks went to church. I stayed home purposely. I was making breakfast in the kitchen when Harley walked in.

He hadn't expected to find me there. His eyes looked away from mine, and he was ready to head back into the living room when I said, "Want some eggs?"

"I got one on my chin," he murmured, "thanks to you."

"Nothing like they've all got. You're a good fighter."

"I guess with my big mouth I'd *better* be. Right, Connor?"

He folded his hands across his chest and gave me this sheepish grin.

"Right!" I agreed.

"OK?" he said, and then quickly, "I'll make us toast. I can do that."

End of discussion, and we never spoke of it again.

Harley didn't make another slip after that.

He wouldn't move back into my bedroom, even though I told him we should take turns. I thought Jitz Rossi would want to even up the score, but instead he tried to get him on the wrestling team since we needed to beat Ithaca, the all-time champions. . . . Harley said he only went in for the martial arts. They weren't big at Cortland High.

Finally, his uncle got back and sent for him.

A month after he left, I got a postcard from Madison.

All it said was, "Thanks, Connor."

I keep wishing I hadn't said all that stuff about him giving me back my room and not taking my socks et cetera. I keep remembering how he took his folks' photograph out to the sleeping porch the first night he spent there. And I can't forget that Sunday morning. I'd feel better if I'd told him calmly what I'd hollered at him in anger.

I should have had the guts to say more.

Maybe he got it, finally . . . or maybe someone in Wisconsin will do him a favor and level with him.

But maybe not, too. And that's what keeps me awake some nights.

⋇ 3 ⋇

Oh, Yes You Will!

"I Will Not Think of Maine"

There are times when a writer writes a short story without knowing where the idea came from.

I am not very interested in the occult, and the only time I was ever in Maine was for a twenty-four-hour visit when I was to speak at a luncheon.

I cannot even remember when I first became acquainted with the word *revenant*, which means "one who returns from the dead." It is not a common word, and it is not in most dictionaries.

Originally, this story was called "The Revenant," for when I sat down and began writing it, I had no plans to include anything about the state of Maine. The revenant in the story was not named Maine then, either.

With an eerie energy, the story of a boy who came back from the dead began taking shape.

The ending was a surprise, even to me. Once it came about, I had to rewrite to give the story a tighter fit. That was when I named the central character Maine.

This story taught me something I sensed as a younger writer but distrusted as an older professional:

When you begin a short story, you don't always have to know what it's about. Some stories come to you as you go along. Maybe you have nothing more than a title or an opening line. Sometimes you have little more than a picture in your head, real or imagined, and your story will be about that.

Once when I was giving a writing workshop in an eighth-grade class, I asked the kids to dream up an opening paragraph for a short story. It could be about anyone or anything, and it didn't need a middle or an ending.

A thirteen-year-old boy named Rudy wrote something that began: *He looks in windows.*

Rudy went on to say that sometimes the moon was out, or a dog was barking, it was pouring rain or "he" was on a fire escape and almost slipped. It was a spooky paragraph. No name, age, or description of the main character.

The teacher took me aside and said, "He's new here. He usually turns in blank pieces of paper, so this is a surprise. But it makes me nervous, too."

When Rudy came up to get his A+ paper, he said, defensively, "It's not about me. It's about my brother."

"What do you think he's looking for, Rudy?"

"He's looking to see how other people live. We lived in our car last summer."

"There's a story," I said. "Could you write about that?"

"I can't write stuff when I'm in it," he said.

"Then don't, but keep on writing, because you're good."

"But we're assigned things like 'My Summer' or 'My Favorite Place' or 'A Perfect Holiday,'" he said.

"Try writing in the third person," I told him.

A lot of us "can't write stuff" when we're in it.

Some writers never write about themselves in the first person.

Maybe Rudy's story *was* really about his brother, but maybe he had learned a great writer's trick: Write about yourself as though someone else is describing you.

Another trick is to just sit down and see who's there, as I did when I found Maine.

❃ I Will Not ❃ Think of Maine

You'd think he'd be pale, that he'd come from the shadows, that I'd never see him very clearly, but Maine stepped into the kitchen on a sunny Saturday morning looking the same way he always did.

So I said, "I must be dreaming."

I'd dreamed he'd come back maybe a dozen times since his death, but it had been months since I'd had that dream.

In it he always looked sad. He always said, "I'm so sorry, Zoë. I didn't mean to go that way."

"You couldn't help it," I'd say. "You were so wild, Maine. You weren't like other kids."

Then I'd wake up. I'd feel full of him again. I'd remember how he stood across my room in the dream, with his long hair and his beautiful face, the one skull earring he always wore, the tattoo of the white pinecone and tassel on his arm, the blue-and-white sweatband on his forehead, like the blue and white of his eyes. I'd remember the low purr of his chuckle when something pleased him.

"I dreamed of Maine again," I'd tell my brother.

"Forget Maine, will you, please? He nearly killed Daddy."

Then there he was in our kitchen one summer morning, big as life. Nothing about him said death.

"Are you a ghost, Maine?"

He laughed hard, but it was not a happy sound, not like another boy's laughter. He slapped his knee where his jeans were torn, his hands filled with rings, those silver bracelets he liked jangling down one arm.

He said, "We don't use the word 'ghost.' We don't haunt houses or that sort of thing. We call ourselves revenants."

"I never heard that word."

"A revenant is someone who comes back."

Then he did what he always used to do, and it would make my mother furious. He opened the refrigerator door, reached in for the carton of orange juice, put it up to his lips, tossed his head back, and took a long gulp.

"I can't believe it's really you," I finally said.

"Your loving pretend brother is back. Am I your dream come true, Zoë?"

"I guess." I was a little embarrassed to admit it. I *had* thought of him that way. But even though Maine and I weren't related, my family had adopted him, and called him "Son." So now I had two brothers.

My family would never have let me date Maine Foremann under any circumstances, not just because he was family. But also because he was different from other boys. He looked like some dark, edgy character out of an old English novel filled with moors and dungeons.

Back then girls hung out in groups nights, often colliding with boys who did the same.

I could never think of anything to say.

The boys weren't big conversationalists, either.

My mother used to say, "Don't you know why Nelson Rider calls you up all the time, Zoë? He's trying to find the words to ask you out."

"All he talks about is acting in the school plays."

"Invite him over. You'll see."

"What would we do?"

"What do you do when you spend time with Maine?"

"That's different," I said. "I always know what to say to Maine."

The truth was, we hadn't talked that much. But I felt close to him. I felt in some secret way he had the same feeling about me, even though he never said so. I looked out at life through my big thick glasses and waited for things to change.

I was always a major daydreamer, even losing track of what went on in movies I'd watch, because I was thinking of what I'd say one day when Maine came into the theater and just sat down in the empty seat next to me.

Maybe I'd say, "What are you doing here?"

Maybe he'd say, "Well, I knew you were in here so I bought a ticket."

And I'd say . . . never mind what I'd say, or what he'd say. If I had all the hours back I'd spent daydreaming about that sort of thing, I'd be the same age I was then. Thirteen. That was my style, age thirteen. I was waiting for Maine to speak up, and tell me what was in his heart.

Mostly, Maine hung out with my real brother, Carl.

They were both fifteen and neither one was that interested in girls yet.

They liked skateboarding together. They'd go

over to Heartsunk Hill and show off. Carl said Maine was a daredevil, so much so sometimes Carl thought he was a little crazy. He said it with a tone of admiration, mostly, but occasionally he sounded exasperated, as though Maine had gone too far . . . like the time Maine brought some beer home he'd gotten an older boy to buy for him. My folks were down at the movies.

He'd shrugged and said, "Your mom doesn't like me drinking your orange juice so I brought my own refreshments."

Carl told him, "You can drink our orange juice, just don't drink from the container. Put it in a glass."

"I've got my own drink now."

"Don't drink it here or I'll be grounded," Carl said.

Maine had a six-pack with him.

He drank it out in the backyard hammock, singing songs by himself. He got louder and sillier, and the cats ran inside and hid under the bed, and the dog wouldn't stop barking at him.

Then he got really sick. I never saw anyone so sick and sorry, and when my folks got back my father had to put him to bed.

Neither of my folks stayed mad at him. Next day, Mom just said, "That boy is so lost, Zoë. I don't know if we're enough to make up for all that's happened to him. But you're a good sister to him, honey."

"I don't think of him as my brother," I said.

She changed the subject. "Carl says Nelson Rider's in the school play."

"When isn't he? He calls me up and says things like 'Boy, is my part hard! I've got more lines than anyone.' What am I supposed to say to that?"

"Say, 'Congratulations!' Or say, 'Tell me about the play.' "

"We're all going to see the play, so I'll know what it's about soon."

"What would you say if Maine said, 'Boy, is my part hard!'?"

"Maine wouldn't be in a school play," I said. "That's not his style."

"Oh, I saw his style last night. Your father and I came along right in time for the upchucking."

"That's not fair," I said. "And Nelson Rider's ears stick out."

Maine seemed so innocent when he'd sit with me and tell me things he'd like to do someday. He'd say he was going back to Maine where he was born, and he was going to live in the woods near a cliff over-looking the ocean.

None of the other boys at school liked Maine. He'd come to us in his freshman year when his parents moved to our town. He'd never connected with a crowd. He shaved his whole head once and painted a Happy face on top, with tears dropping from its eyes. He made no effort to get better than passing grades, even though he knew the answers to most every question any teacher asked in class. He'd tell us school bored him. He complained he missed the weather in Bangor, where he used to live. He missed the bitter cold. Even in freezing weather he wouldn't wear gloves or a scarf, or ear-muffs like the rest of us.

In falling snow I'd see him with his jacket open, shirt unbuttoned, boots laced only halfway—he had a flair. I envied him that. My mother told me flair and fashion didn't just *happen*—you had to create it for yourself. You had to work at it.

I always doubted there was much I could do with myself. I threw on my clothes and tried not to look in a mirror because I'd see that I was hopeless.

One day, when the family was new in town, Maine's mother showed up at our house looking for him. She was beautiful, and she was driving this white Porsche convertible, and she said, "Tell him his father and I are going to California tonight and we'd like to see him before we go."

Maine could hear her. He was hiding in the hall closet.

When she left, I said, "Wow! Is that your mom? Was that her car?"

Maine said, "You're very impressionable, Zoë."

Carl said, "What do they do in California?"

"They sun themselves," Maine said.

"What does your father do for a living?"

"He makes movies," Maine said.

"Wow!" I said.

"Really?" Carl asked.

"Horror movies," he said. "B movies. . . . You'd think he didn't have a brain in his head."

"But she looks so glitzy, Maine, and she's nice!"

"I'm not close to them. They're always gone."

"Do you ever go with them?" I asked.

"I prefer not to be seen with them," said Maine.

He'd break me up saying things like that. He was cool. I always wanted to be like that: cool.

That morning he showed up in our kitchen, Maine said, "I came back for a reason, Zoë."

"To say you're sorry for almost running over my father? He was in the hospital for months, and he still limps."

"I shouted at him to get out of the way, Zoë! I tried to brake, but it was too late."

"But you were going down *our* driveway in *our* car!"

"I know where I was, Zoë. One thing you always know is where you were when you were born, and where you were when you died." He leaned over and looked out the window. "I died right down the street by that oak tree." Then he socked his palm with his fist. "Pow!" he said. "What a crash! I never drove a car before!"

"I kept dreaming you came back, Maine, and now here you are!"

"Not for long," he said. "I came back on a Saturday morning when I knew your folks would be out, your brother over on Heartsunk skating, and you'd probably be here alone."

I shivered.

"Don't tremble. I'm not going to hurt you. I just want you to stop dreaming about me. Could you please put me out of your head altogether?"

"How did you know I—"

He cut me off. "We always know because we can't rest if people dream of us. It's been a year now, Zoë. When my family died, I stopped dreaming of them after about a week."

I didn't say the obvious: that he hadn't liked his family, but that I had been crazy about him.

He said, "I had no friends but you and Carl. He's *never* dreamed of me. But you do."

"Yes, I do. Not so much lately, but I definitely do."

"Don't!" Maine said. "I don't want to spend the rest of my time in eternity waiting for you to stop dreaming of me. I want to escape life forever . . . to sleep, finally!"

"It's just that I always felt so close to you, Maine."

"Don't be like my mother. She had this crush on a rock star she'd never even talked to. After he died in a plane crash, she still kept obsessing about him, even after she got married."

I said, "Am I obsessing? I don't think of it *that* way."

He went right on. "Mother dreamed of him all the time. . . . Then when I was born, I was filled with his spirit. I was born a revenant. That's what made me so different."

"But you said you're a revenant *now*?"

"I was then and I am still. Only now I know what I am. After my encounter with that oak tree down the street I got back my eternal memory. Then I knew why I had never warmed to anyone. It's a revenant trait, you see: We don't warm to live people. Our hearts are so ancient and weary. We feel distanced."

"But you felt close to Carl and me."

"He was the only guy at school who could stand me. So I hung around here. But I didn't feel close to anyone. Not even your parents, and particularly not my parents."

I could feel my heart banging under my blouse, but my voice didn't give anything away. I said, "Did your mother know what you were?"

"Yes. She was warned just as I'm warning you. The rock star told her to let go, that if she didn't he'd return in one form or another, as a revenant."

"Your poor mother!"

Maine threw his head back and roared. "That's a good one! How about poor me? . . . Mommy thought it was fascinating. She even told my father. Anyone else would have thought she didn't have all her marbles, but *he* was fascinated, too. I was their little experiment. They became obsessed with the occult. That happens to people. They get a taste of the eternal and they do strange things: go to séances, hang out with others like them, buy Ouija boards, write creepy screenplays. . . . And they found out everything they could about revenants. They found out that we thrive in cold climates, that it's best to name us after a cold place. Best to stamp cold symbols somewhere on us: a pinecone, a snowbird, something like that. It's supposed to keep us calm."

I stared at his tattoo and felt a chill.

Maine said, "They followed all the rules in the beginning, but I wasn't much like her old rock star crush. Every revenant needs a spirit to ride back on, but the resemblance stops there. We go our own way, whether we're flesh or vapor." He shook his head, flashed me one of his lopsided smiles. "They just didn't like me. No one ever really does."

"I did," I said. "I still do."

"It's fading, though. You said so yourself. . . . And that's exactly why I'm here."

Then his blue eyes looked directly into mine. "Say this sentence with me, Zoë, okay?"

"Okay."

"I will not dream of Maine."

"I will not dream of Maine," I said.

"Say it over and over to yourself," he said. "Say good-bye forever."

"Good-bye forever."

I looked away because I didn't want him to see my tears.

When I looked again, Maine Foremann was gone.

The only thing I could find on revenants in our library was one paragraph in an occult book. It said the revenant spirit returns sometimes seen, sometimes unseen. Of all ghosts, revenants were the slickest and trickiest.

And I believed it. For what I could not accept was Maine's claim he did not feel *anything* for me. I told myself it was his way of keeping me from dreaming of him. The only way he could be free was to burst my bubble.

I wanted to be free of him, as well. It was time for me to grow up and get a life. I replaced my thick glasses with contact lenses, began studying *Vogue* when I was at the hairdresser's, even suffered through a performance of *The Sound of Music*, with Nelson Rider singing off-key.

Still . . . although it was fairly long since I had allowed myself to think of Maine for more than a pinch of time, often there was a shadow and a glimpse of a bare arm with a white tassel marked upon it, passing through my dreams.

One summer, Carl was home from college, and he brought a movie from the video store one night.

"Guess who made it?" he said, after dinner. "Maine Foremann's father."

"That poor crazy kid!" our father said. "May he rest in peace."

"Amen!" I said.

I didn't want to see *Born on Cold Nights*.

I went into the kitchen and stacked the dishes in the dishwasher. Carl would shout at me from time to time, "Zoë! Come in and watch this! This is weird, Zoë!"

"I'm going out."

"Again?" my father called in to me.

"Again," I said. "And I'm late. People are waiting for me."

"Zoë!" Carl wouldn't give up. "Hey, Zoë! Don't think of a yellow elephant!"

"What is that supposed to mean?" I peered around the corner at my brother.

"This guy playing the revenant says if you tell someone not to do something, they can't help doing it."

Just for a moment, I listened.

We are revenants with spirits that long to return as revenants. You humans with one life cannot know the joy of life again and again and yet again. Our desire is to return, and your dreaming makes it possible. But what if you stop dreaming of us? How can we prevent that?

My father shook his head. "Well, we did our best for the boy. But I have to admit that I don't miss him. Do you, Zoë?"

I just shrugged as though it wasn't a question that needed an answer.

Then I left the house, thinking of a yellow elephant, and hearing the low purr of a chuckle somewhere in the vapors of that summer evening.

❧ 4 ❧

Recurrent
Themes

"The Green Killer"

A prolific writer is liable to realize one day that certain characters and situations recur in her work. She didn't plan it that way; it happened.

Lawrence Durrell said each writer gets only one deck of cards, and he plays them over and over in different ways.

It was many years before I realized that one of my recurring themes is the relationship between two brothers, or two young men who are related or living together under the same roof.

In "Like Father, Like Son" Harley comes to live

with Connor, and in "I Will Not Think of Maine" Maine is adopted by Carl's family. In "The Author" Peter is jealous of his stepbrother, whom he calls Tom Terrific. And in "The Green Killer" the focus is on Alan's envy of his cousin Blaze.

Until I began working on this collection, I was not even aware of these similarities.

Although I have two brothers, there is a sixteen-year age difference between them, they lived far apart geographically, and I was never aware of any stress they might have caused each other.

Another recurrent theme in my short stories and novels is the have vs. the have-not.

Both were favorite themes of Charles Dickens. Rather than imagine some psychological reasons for playing my cards as I do, I prefer to blame Dickens, whose novels my father read aloud to me when I was a child.

In "The Green Killer" the two themes are combined. Oddly enough, just as Maine came back from the dead in "I Will Not Think of Maine," Blaze, in this story, has his own way of winning retribution from the grave.

ᕽ The *ᕽ* Green Killer

"Be nice to him," my father said. "He's your cousin, after all."

"He takes my things."

"Don't be silly, Alan. What of yours could Blaze possibly want? He has everything . . . *everything*," my father added with a slight tone of disdain, for we all knew how spoiled my cousin was.

But he did take my things. Not things he wanted because he needed them, but little things like a seashell I'd saved and polished, an Indian head nickel I'd found, a lucky stone shaped like a star. Every time he came from New York City with his family for a visit, some little thing of mine was missing after they left.

We were expecting them for Thanksgiving that year. It was our turn to do the holiday dinner with all our relatives. Everyone would be crowded into our dining room with extra card tables brought up from the cellar, and all sorts of things borrowed from the next-door neighbors: folding chairs, extra serving platters, one of those giant coffee pots that could serve twenty . . . on and on.

It was better when it was their turn and everyone trooped into New York for a gala feast in their Fifth Avenue apartment overlooking Central Park. They had a doorman to welcome us, a cook to make the turkey dinner, maids to serve us.

Blaze's father was the CEO of Dunn Industry. My father was the principal of Middle Grove High School on Long Island. About the only thing the two brothers had in common was a son apiece: brilliant, dazzling Blaze Dunn, seventeen; and yours truly, Alan Dunn, sixteen, average.

But that was a Thanksgiving no one in the family would ever get to enjoy or forget. An accident on the Long Island Expressway caused the cherry-black Mercedes to overturn, and my cousin Blaze was killed instantly.

I had mixed emotions the day, months later, when I was invited into New York to take what I wanted of Blaze's things.

Did I want to wear those cashmere sweaters and wool jackets and pants I'd always envied, with their Ralph Lauren and Calvin Klein labels? The shoes—even the shoes fit me, British-made Brooks Brothers Church's. Suits from Paul Stuart. Even the torn jeans and salty denim jackets had a hyper-elegant "preppy" tone.

Yes!

Yes, I wanted to have them! It would make up for all the times my stomach had turned over with envy when he walked into a room, and the niggling awareness always there that my cousin flaunted his riches before me with glee. And all the rest—his good looks (Blaze was almost beautiful with his tanned perfect face, long eyelashes, green eyes, shiny black hair); and of course he was a straight-A student. He was at ease in any social situation. More than at ease. He was an entertainer, a teller of stories, a boy who could make you listen and laugh. Golden. He was a golden boy. My own mother admitted it. Special, unique, a winner—all of those things I'd heard said about Blaze. Even the name, never mind it was his mother's maiden name. Blaze Dunn. I used to imagine one day I'd see it up on the marquee of some Broadway theater, or on a book cover, or at the bottom of a painting in the Museum of Modern Art. He'd wanted to be an actor, a writer, a painter. His only problem, he had always said, was deciding which talent to stress.

While I packed up garment bags full of his clothes, I pictured him leering down from that up above where we imagine the dead watching us. I thought of him smirking at the sight of me there in his room, imagined him saying, "It's the only way *you'd* ever luck out like this, Snail!" He used to call me that. Snail. It was because I'd take naps when he was visiting. I couldn't help it. I'd get exhausted by him. I'd curl up in my room and hope he'd be gone when I'd wake up. . . . He said snails slept a lot, too. He'd won a prize once for an essay he'd written about snails. He'd described how snails left a sticky discharge under them as they moved, and he claimed that because of it a snail could crawl along the edge of a razor without cutting itself. . . . He'd have the whole dining table enthralled while he repeated things like that from his prizewinning essays. And while I retreated to my room to sleep— that was when he took my things.

All right. He took my things; I took *his* things.

❖ ❖ ❖

I thought I might feel weird wearing his clothes, and even my mother wondered if I'd be comfortable in them. It was my father who thundered, "Ridiculous! Take advantage of your advantages! It's an inheritance, of sorts. You don't turn down *money* that's left you!"

Not only did I not feel all that weird in Blaze's clothes, I began to take on a new confidence. I think I even walked with a new, sure step. I know I became more outgoing, you might even say more popular. Not dazzling, no, not able to hold a room spellbound while I tossed out some information about the habits of insects, but in my own little high-school world out on Long Island I wasn't the old average Alan Dunn plodding along snaillike anymore. That spring I got elected to the prom committee, which decides the theme for the big end-of-the-year dance, and I even found the courage to ask Courtney Sweet out.

The only magic denied me by my inheritance seemed to be whatever it would take to propel me from being an average student with grades slipping down too often into Cs and Ds, up into Blaze's A and A+ status. My newfound confidence had swept me into a social whirl that was affecting my studies. I was almost flunking science.

When I finally unpacked a few boxes of books and trivia that Blaze's mother had set aside for me, I found my seashell, my Indian head nickel, and my lucky stone. . . . And other things: a thin gold girl's bracelet, a silver key ring from Tiffany, initials H.J.K. A school ring of some sort with a ruby stone. A medal with two golf clubs crossed on its face. A lot of little things like that . . . and then a small red leather notebook the size of a playing card.

In very tiny writing inside, Blaze had listed initials, dates, and objects this way:

A.D.	December 25	Shell
H.K.	March 5	Key ring
A.D.	November 28	Indian nickel

He had filled several pages.

Obviously, I had not been the only one whose things Blaze had swiped. It was nothing personal.

As I flipped the pages, I saw more tiny writing in the back of the notebook.

A sentence saying: *"Everything is sweetened by risk."*

Another: *"Old burglars never die, they just steal away. (Ha! Ha!)"*

And: *"I dare, you don't. I have, you won't."*

Even today I wonder why I never told anyone about this. It was not because I wanted to protect Blaze or to leave the glorified memories of him undisturbed. I suppose it comes down to what I found at the bottom of one of the boxes.

The snail essay was there, and there was a paper written entirely in French. There was a composition describing a summer he had spent on the Cape, probably one of those "What I Did Last Summer" assignments unimaginative teachers give at the beginning of fall terms. . . . I did not bother to read beyond the opening sentences, which were "The Cape has always bored me to death for everyone goes there to have fun, clones with their golf clubs, tennis rackets, and volleyballs! There are no surprises on the Cape, no mysteries, no danger."

None of it interested me until I found "The Green Killer." It was an essay with an A+ marked on it, and handwriting saying, "As usual, Blaze, you excel!"

The title made it sound like a Stephen King fantasy, but the essay was a description of an ordinary praying mantis . . . a neat and gory picture of the sharp spikes on his long legs that shot out, dug into an insect, and *snap* went his head!

"You think it is praying," Blaze had written, *"but it is waiting to kill!"*

My heart began pounding as I read, not because of any bloodthirsty instinct in me, but because an essay for science was due, and here was *my* chance to excel!

Blaze had gone to a private school in New York that demanded students handwrite their essays, so I carefully copied the essay into my computer, making a little bargain with Blaze's ghost as I printed it out: *I will not tell on you in return for borrowing your handiwork. Fair is fair. Your golden reputation will stay untarnished, while my sad showing in science will be enhanced through you.*

"The Green Killer" was an enormous hit. Mr. Van Fleet, our teacher, read it aloud, while I sat there beaming in Blaze's torn Polo jeans and light blue cashmere sweater. Nothing of mine had ever been read in class before. I had never received an A.

After class, Mr. Van Fleet informed me that he was entering the essay in a statewide science contest, and he congratulated me, adding, "You've changed, Alan. I don't mean just this essay—but *you*. Your personality. We've all noticed it." Then he gave me a friendly punch, and grinned slyly. "Maybe Courtney Sweet has inspired you."

And she was waiting for me by my locker, looking

all over my face as she smiled at me, purring her congratulations.

Ah, Blaze, I thought, *finally, my dear cousin, you're my boy . . . and your secret is safe with me. That's our deal.*

Shortly after my essay was sent off to the science competition, Mr. Van Fleet asked me to stay after class again.

"Everyone," he said, "was impressed with 'The Green Killer,' Alan. Everyone agreed it was remarkable."

"Thank you," I said, unbuttoning my Ralph Lauren blazer, breathing a sigh of pleasure, rocking back and forth in my Church's loafers.

"And why not?" Mr. Van Fleet continued. "It was copied word for word from an essay written by Isaac Asimov. One of the judges spotted it immediately."

So Blaze was Blaze—even dead he'd managed to take something from me once again.

⋇ 5 ⋇

Guess Who's Coming to Your School!

"The Author"

One of the things I like best is visiting schools and getting the chance to talk with kids.

Sometimes, though, I wonder if the kids are as pleased as I am.

Certain teachers pass out Author Evaluation Sheets among the students and, at my request, send the comments on to me. I learn a lot from them, and occasionally I'm humbled.

One of the answers to the question *What did you like most about Ms. Kerr's talk?* came from a boy named Wallace.

Sitting next to Brenda, Wallace wrote.

Years ago in the Midwest, as I walked with a teacher through the parking lot upon my arrival at her school, she noticed all the boys were wearing dark suits and ties.

She said, "They know you're the guest of honor today! Why, look what they've done! They've dressed up for you!"

I wanted to believe it, but a little voice of reason deep inside me whispered, "Get real, Ms. Kerr!"

I spoke in assembly, and then later to a smaller group, where I had a chance to answer and ask questions.

"How come you boys are all in suits and ties?"

A girl said, "We're all in skirts, too."

"What's the reason?" I persisted.

"To honor Kurt Cobain," a boy shouted out.

That famous rock star had committed suicide the day before my arrival.

So I earned my slight skepticism about my school visits honestly.

This short story reflects some of that feeling.

⁊ The Author ⁊

B efore the author comes to school, we all have
to write him, saying we are glad he is coming
and we like his books.

That is Ms. Terripelli's idea. She is our English
teacher and she was the one who first got the idea
to have real, live authors visit Leighton Middle
School.

She wants the author to feel welcome.

You are my favorite author, I write.

I have never read anything he's written.

Please send me an autographed picture, I write. I am
sure this will raise my English grade, something I

need desperately, since it is not one of my best subjects.

The truth is: I have best friends and best clothes and best times, but not best subjects.

I am going to be an author, too, someday, I write, surprised to see the words pop up on the screen. But I am writing on the computer in the school library and there is something wonderful about the way any old thought can become little green letters in seconds, which you can erase with one touch of your finger.

I don't push WordEraser, however.

I like writing that I am going to be an author.

The person I am writing to is Peter Sand.

My name happens to be Peter too.

Peter Sangetti.

I might shorten my name to Peter Sang, when I become an author, I write. *Then maybe people will buy my books by mistake, thinking they are getting yours. (Ha! Ha!)*

Well, I write, *before this turns into a book and you sell it for money, I will sign off, but I will be looking for you when you show up at our school.*

I sign it *Sincerely,* although that's not exactly true.

The night before the author visit, my dad comes over to see me. My stepfather and my mother have gone off to see my stepbrother, Tom, in Leighton

High School's version of *The Sound of Music*.

To myself, and sometimes to my mother, I call him Tom Terrific. Naturally, he has the lead in the musical. He is Captain von Trapp. If they ever make the Bible into a play, he will be God.

I like him all right, but I am tired of playing second fiddle to him always. He is older, smarter, and better looking, and his last name is Prince. Really.

I can't compete with him.

It's funny, because the first words out of my dad's mouth that night are, "I can't compete with that."

He is admiring the new CD audio system my stepfather had ordered from the Sharper Image catalog. It is an Aiwa with built-in BBE sound.

"It's really for Tom Terrific," I say, but it is in the living room, not Tom's bedroom, and Dad knows my CD collection is my pride and joy.

I suppose just as I try to compete with Tom Terrific, my dad tries to compete with Thomas Prince, Sr. . . . Both of us are losing the game, it seems. My dad is even out of work just now, although it is our secret . . . not to be shared with my mom or stepfather.

The plant where he worked was closed. He'd have to move out of the state to find the same kind of job he had there, and he doesn't want to leave me.

"I'm not worried about you," I lie. And then I hurry to change the subject, and tell him about the author's visit, next day.

He smiles and shakes his head. "Funny. I once wanted to be a writer."

"I never knew that."

"Sure. One time I got this idea for a story about our cat. She was always sitting in the window of our apartment building, looking out. She could never get out, but she'd sit there, and I'd think it'd be her dream come true if she could see a little of the world! Know what I mean, Pete?"

"Sure I do." I also know my dad always wished he could travel. He is the only person I've ever known who actually reads *National Geographic*.

He laughs. "So I invented a story about the day she got out. Here was her big chance to run around the block!"

"What happened?"

"A paper bag fell from one of the apartments above ours. It landed right on Petunia's head. She ran around the block, all right, but she didn't see a thing."

Both of us roar at the idea, but deep down I don't think it is that hilarious, considering it is my dad who dreamed it up.

What's he think—that he'll never see the world?

Never have his dreams come true?

"Hey, what's the matter?" he says. "You look down in the dumps suddenly."

"Not me," I say.

"Aw, that was a dumb story," he says. "Stupid!"

"It was fine," I say.

"No, it wasn't," he says. "I come over here and say things to spoil your evening. You'd rather hear your music."

"No, I wouldn't," I say, but he is getting up to go.

We are losing touch not living in the same house anymore.

Whenever I go over to his apartment, he spends a lot of time apologizing for it. It is too small. It isn't very cheerful. It needs a woman's touch. I want to tell him that if he'd just stop pointing out all the things wrong with it, I'd like it fine . . . but it is turning out that we aren't great talkers anymore. I don't say everything on my mind anymore.

He shoots me a mock punch at the door and tells me that next week he'll get some tickets to a hockey game. Okay with me? I say he doesn't have to, thinking of the money, and he says I know it's not like going to the World Series or anything. I'd gone to the World Series the year before with my stepfather.

"Let up," I mumble.

"What?" he says.

"Nothing."

He says, "I heard you, Pete. You're right. You're right."

Next day, waiting for me out front is Ms. Terripelli.

"He asked for you, Pete! You're going to be Mr. Sand's guide for the day."

"Why me?" I ask.

"Because you want to be a writer?" She looks at me and I look at her.

"Oh, that," I say.

"You never told the class that," she says.

"It's too personal."

"Do you write in secret, Pete?"

"I have a lot of ideas," I say.

"Good for you!" says Ms. Terripelli, and she hands me a photograph of Peter Sand. It is autographed. It also has written on it, "Maybe someday I'll be asking for yours, so don't change your name. Make me wish it was mine, instead."

"What does all that mean?" Ms. Terripelli asks me.

"Just author stuff," I say.

I put the picture in my locker and go to the faculty lounge to meet him.

He is short and plump, with a mustache. He looks like a little colonel of some sort, because he has this booming voice and a way about him that makes you feel he knows his stuff.

"I never write fantasy," he says. "I write close to home. When you read my books, you're reading about something that happened to me! . . . Some authors write both fantasy and reality!"

At the end of his talks he answers all these questions about his books and he autographs paperback copies.

I hang out with him the whole time.

We don't get to say much to each other until lunch.

The school doesn't dare serve him what we get in the cafeteria, so they send out for heros, and set up a little party for him in the lounge.

The principal shows up, and some librarians from the Leighton Town Library.

When we do get a few minutes to talk he asks me what I am writing.

I say, "We had this cat, Petunia, who was always looking out the window . . ."

He is looking right into my eyes as though he is fascinated, and I finish the story.

"Wow!" he says. "Wow!"

"It's sort of sad," I say.

"It has heart and it has humor, Pete," he says. "The best stories always do."

His last session is in the school library, and members of the town are invited.

About fifty people show up.

He talks about his books for a while, and then he starts talking about me.

He tells the story about Petunia. He calls it wistful and amusing, and he says anyone who can think up a story like that knows a lot about the world already.

I get a lot of pats on the back afterward, and Ms. Terripelli says, "Well, you've had quite a day for yourself, Pete."

By this time I am having trouble looking her in the eye.

Things are a little out of hand, but what the heck—he is on his way to the airport and back to Maine, where he lives. What did it hurt that I told a few fibs?

Next day, the *Leighton Lamplighter* has the whole story. I hadn't even known there was a reporter present. There is the same photograph Peter Sand has given to me, and there is my name in the article about the author visit.

My name. Dad's story of Petunia, with no mention of Dad.

"Neat story!" says Tom Terrific.

My stepfather says if I show him a short story all finished and ready to send out somewhere, he'll think about getting me a word processor.

"I don't write for gain," I say.

Mom giggles. "You're a wiseguy, Pete."

"Among other things," I say.

Like a liar, I am thinking. Like a liar and a cheat.

When Dad calls, I am waiting for the tirade.

He has a bad temper. He is the type who leaves nothing unsaid when he blows. I expect him to blow blue: he does when he loses his temper. He comes up with slang that would knock the socks off the Marine Corps.

"Hey, Pete," he says, "you really liked my story, didn't you?"

"Too much, I guess. That's why you didn't get any credit."

"What's mine is yours, kid. I've always told you that."

"I went off the deep end, I guess, telling him I want to be a writer."

"An apple never falls far from the tree, Pete. That was my ambition when I was your age."

"Yeah, you told me. . . . But *me*. What do I know?"

"You have a good imagination, son. And you convinced Peter Sand what you were saying was true."

"I'm a good liar, I guess."

"Or a good storyteller. . . . Which one?"

Why does he have to say which one?

Why does he have to act so pleased to have given me something?

The story of Petunia isn't really a gift. I realize that now. It was more like a loan.

I can tell the story, just as my dad told it to me, but when I try to turn myself from a liar into a storyteller, it doesn't work on paper.

I fool around with it for a while. I try.

The thing is: fantasy is not for me.

I finally find out what is when I come up with a first sentence, which begins:

Before the author comes to school, we all have to write him, saying we are glad he is coming and we like his books.

You see, I am an author who writes close to home.

NOVELS
(AND
AUTOBIOGRAPHY)

I SOLD MY FIRST NOVEL WHEN I WAS TWENTY-THREE years old, one year after I'd graduated from the University of Missouri. I was working for Fawcett Publications, and they were launching a new paperback line called Gold Medal Books.

"I could write one of these," I told the editor, and when he asked me what I'd write about, I answered, "Sorority life at a big university. What goes on during rush week, and what happens to pledges after a sorority takes them in."

"Give me an outline and a first chapter, and we'll see," he told me.

I went to an art supply store and bought a large blank white poster.

Across the top I wrote NAME, AGE, DESCRIPTION, BACKGROUND, HABITS, BEGINNING, END.

I listed my main characters, almost as though I was casting a movie. Sometimes under DESCRIPTION I would even put down the name of a real movie star. Under BACKGROUND I would write things like "Raised on a farm in Bolivar, Missouri," or "Rich girl from New York City."

Under HABITS I would write, "A loner who reads poetry, misses hometown boyfriend and writes him every night." Or "Tries out for all the school plays, was voted 'Most beautiful in boarding school,' is a snob."

BEGINNING described what was going on with each character as the novel began. "Forced to go on blind dates with fraternity boys. Misses boyfriend. Is shy and unhappy." And "Made to room with farm girl, makes fun of her, is very popular with frat boys."

END dealt with where the characters were when the novel was finished. "Best friend now with snob roommate, but hometown boyfriend has another girl." Then "Pregnant, must leave college."

My novel chart gave me a good start. My characters were all in place, and I knew what I wanted to happen to them.

My first chapter came spilling out. The editor liked it, and I received an advance. I was on my way.

I learned very quickly that things changed in between BEGINNING and END. A novel takes on its own energy, and often the characters just won't go exactly where you want them to, so some ENDs were different from what I'd thought they would be.

But the whole idea of the novel chart paid off. There, right in front of me as I sat working at my typewriter, was the world I was creating. I had only to glance up to remember that "Marilyn" looked like a young Bette Davis, that "Alan" was an Alpha Tau Omega frat boy who chain-smoked Camel cigarettes, and that "Ellen" had red hair and was a kleptomaniac.

I no longer need a novel chart before I sit down at my computer, but for many years the highlight of starting a new book was getting out a fresh poster and casting my characters.

A novel gives you a legitimate way to have a little world of your own creation. While you're writing it, you're escaping into it, not only as you sit down to do your daily stint but often while you're on a walk, at a party, driving in your car, watching a movie, or falling asleep at the end of the day.

Like someone slightly crazy, you hear voices in your head and see visions no one else does.

You are amazed to discover that this world you brought into being becomes very real, and often what you thought you were controlling begins to control you.

The famous writer W. Somerset Maugham wrote: "There are three rules for writing a novel. Unfortunately no one knows what they are."

Maybe no one really can tell another writer how to write a novel, but here are some tips from my experience:

Read a lot! Don't expect to run in a race when

you don't know whom you're running against. Then write the kind of novel you like to read.

Your first three chapters hook your reader into your story. Work hard on them, rewrite, get them as good as you can. After about thirty pages, you should find your voice (or voices), and when you do, your characters will begin to speak and act on their own.

Try to provide enough suspense at the end of each chapter to make the reader want to go on to the next.

Don't tell everything too soon. A good story doesn't rush at the reader; it unfolds gradually.

In the beginning, expect to sweat! Novel writing is hard work! Don't turn against yourself or your material. Recognize how brave you are. Respect yourself and reward yourself.

Besides perfecting your way with words, work on the second most important skill: Persistence. Not only do you need it to finish your book, but after you finish, you need it to get your book into the right hands.

Whatever you do, *don't* talk your ideas away. A lot of people can talk a good story, but you want to write one. So keep it to yourself as you work.

Every novel has a story behind it. The time to tell it is *after* you've written it.

Here are some of mine.

❖ 1 ❖

What if?

Gentlehands

One summer I moved from New York City to a resort town on the tip of Long Island. East Hampton changes in the summer months from a sleepy small town to a bustling vacation spot.

I'd bought a house next door to a policeman's family. Bobby, the oldest boy, was sixteen and worked in an ice-cream parlor called Mellow Mouth.

Into that shop strolled a summer teenager who took a good look at Bobby, decided he was a hunk, and asked him out.

To give you an idea of the difference between

them, he had just received a new ten-speed bike from his dad, and she had just been given a new Porsche by hers.

He would be going back to high school, in the fall, to begin his senior year. She would start her freshman year at Bryn Mawr. He was barely passing French. She had learned to speak French, German, and Spanish fluently, in the boarding school she'd just graduated from in Europe.

Bobby's mother said, "She's going to mop up the floor with you, son. She's not our class."

Her mother said, "Don't get involved with a 'townie,' honey. You'll be meeting college boys in a few months."

But nearly every night, I would hear the beep of her horn outside Bobby's house. Sometimes she was behind the wheel of her Porsche; other times she drove her mother's little English Jensen, or her father's Mercedes convertible. Bobby would run out to the car, and off they would go.

Often I would put aside my reading to answer one of Bobby's questions when he would knock at my door.

What should he wear when he went to her mansion on the ocean for dinner? What fork should he pick up? Her father loved opera. What could I tell Bobby about opera? What could he take her mother when they had gardens tended by a gardener, and boxes of Swiss chocolates, mints, and mixed nuts set out on tables everywhere?

Since I had just moved from New York City, he thought I might be sophisticated enough to know the answers . . . and anyway, when he asked his mother the same questions, she'd say, "We're not teaching you snob things," because she didn't have the answers.

The more in love he became with her, the more he realized he was a fish out of water in her fancy crowd. They all owned cars, dressed like models for Polo ads (her trademark was to dress all in one color), and passed around pot as they sat by her swimming pool in view of the ocean. Pot, in Bobby's house, was a "controlled substance." His policeman father would have grounded him until Labor Day if he had known what kind of crowd Bobby was traveling with.

I like to write stories about haves and have-nots. I wondered if Fate hadn't planted me right next door to great material. I began to think about this love affair between a "townie" and a rich summer girl. It might make a good little story . . . but it seemed to me that was about all it would turn out to be: a little story.

❄ ❄ ❄

That summer there was something else very much on my mind. Imagine this: A nineteen-year-old man is known for two things: his dazzling looks and his terrible cruelty.

In reports I read about him, he was described as one of the most sadistic Nazi officers in Auschwitz, a concentration camp where there were many Jewish women from Italy.

After his evening meal he would often go down to the yard of the camp and wait for the women to return from a twelve-hour day of forced labor. He would greet them smiling, as an opera played from speakers. Then he would announce that they were to dance and sing for him.

Most of them could barely walk, they were so tired and undernourished. Many of them fell to the ground. They were the ones he sicced his dogs on.

This tall blond young commandant with the light-blue eyes, in the smart Nazi uniform, had many other diabolical "games" to play on those in his charge.

I began to read everything I could find about him, trying to discover what made someone that way.

You always imagine you can find an answer. An unhappy childhood, perhaps. Someone who was cruel to him. Maybe a low intelligence that would make him unable to perceive what he was doing.

Although this man had been raised in a strict religious family, he had not entered the priesthood as they had hoped he would. Lured by the new, powerful Nazi regime, he became an SS officer. Popular with his comrades and engaged to be married, he was as intelligent as he was attractive. There was nothing in his background to suggest a reason for his barbarity, or for the pleasure he took in torturing inmates.

I spent the summer reading Holocaust literature, curious about the nature of these Germans who supervised the concentration camps.

One book that was part of my research was called *WANTED: The Search for Nazis in the United States of America*, by Howard Blum. It was about certain Nazis who had escaped to this country by lying about their part in the Holocaust.

What if there was a way to combine the love story with the story of this young Nazi? He would no longer be young, of course. He would be old enough to be a grandfather.

What if triggers most ideas for novels. It is often the very heart of fiction. You take something real and add to it.

What if Bobby had a grandfather who had once been a Nazi, unbeknownst to Bobby?

What if the family of Bobby's girlfriend had a houseguest who was hunting down the Nazi?

What if this Nazi had had a nickname he was known by in that concentration camp, an ironical name that said everything he was not . . . the way one might call a very tall person "Shorty"?

What about the Italian operas he loved to play, ones like *Tosca*? *Tosca*, with that aria *"O dolci mani,"* translated as *"O sweet hands . . . O gentle hands."*

Gentlehands . . . I had my title.

Some authors name their books after they have written them. I cannot begin until I have the title, and the first line.

I wonder what that summer would have been like if I'd never met Skye Pennington.

Somewhere there is a woman who would now be in her thirties. I don't know if she still dresses all in one color. I doubt very much that she knows a book was written about a certain summer when she dated a "townie." Although her family moved from East Hampton, I borrowed their butler, Peacock (his real name), for this book, and her mother's Jensen, and their home on the ocean.

The beginning of Bobby's romance is described

exactly as it happened, except that the summer girl asked Bobby for the first date. In real life, he was far too shy.

Although my fictional Nazi was nicknamed Gentlehands, I made his real name Frank Trenker. His merciless behavior in Auschwitz came directly from the literature concerning him.

My Nazi hunter, Nick De Lucca, was entirely fictional.

Many people did not like the fact that the Nazi was so handsome and likeable, and that Nick wore ugly yellow-lensed glasses and was snide. We like things to be clear, bad guys to look like bad guys, good guys to look like us.

We would rather distance ourselves from evil. It is more comfortable to believe that the enemy is nothing like we are. When I was growing up during World War II, Nazis were depicted as goose-stepping buffoons, caricatures like those in the old TV sitcom *Hogan's Heroes*.

How, then, to explain the fact that while the world looked away, these inept, obnoxious fools were able to murder six million Jews, along with six million homosexuals, Gypsies, political enemies, and others deemed "unfit" because of mental or physical defects?

Speaking of *What If*: What if the Nazi I read

about had been older, uglier, and dumber? What if he'd had a rotten childhood, was a loner without friends or a fiancée? Would I have been inspired then to begin my research?

Probably not.

Unlike Pogo, the comic-strip hero who declared, "We have met the enemy and he is us," my immediate reaction to the model for Gentlehands was the naive view that Evil is never attractive, intelligent, or inexplicable—when instead, I should have realized it is often, at its most lethal, all three of these things.

What follow are the first three chapters of *Gentlehands*.

from

⤳ Gentlehands ⤵

I wonder what that summer would have been like if I'd never met Skye Pennington. They always seem to have names like that, don't they? Rich, beautiful girls are never named Elsie Pip or Mary Smith. They have these special names and they say them in their particular tones and accents, and my mother was right, I was in over my head or out of my depth, or however she put it. My father said, "She's not our class, Buddy." This conversation the first night I took her out.

I was in the bathroom, pretending to shave. I'm a towhead, like all male Boyles, and at sixteen my beard is not a burden; it's not even a fact.

My mother was just outside, in the hall, pretending to straighten out the linen closet.

Streaker, my five-year-old brother, was around the corner in our bedroom, pretending he could play Yahtzee alone.

My father was using the top of the toilet seat like a chair, while he discussed the matter with me.

"She's not in our class?" I said. "What does that even mean?"

I knew what it meant. It meant we lived year round in Seaville, New York, on a seedy half-acre lot up near the bay, and Skye summered on five ocean-view acres at the other end of town.

Another thing it meant was that my dad was a sergeant in the Seaville police force, and Skye's dad was head of Penn Industries.

"Do you actually pay attention to that stuff?" I said, as if I never did.

"Buddy, that stuff is a fact of life." My mother's voice from the hall. "Sad but true."

"Inge, am I handling this, or are you?" said my father.

"Oh excuse me for living," my mother said.

"I thought you asked me to handle it."

"I asked you to talk to him."

"What is there to talk about?" I said.

"What there is to talk about is where the hell you're spending all your money!"

"Don't get mad at him, Billy," said my mother. "I said to talk to him, not to shout at him."

"It's my money, isn't it? I earned it," I said.

"Since when do you spend your money on clothes?" my father said.

"If you know where I'm spending my money, why do you want to talk about where I'm spending it?" I said.

"You're spending it on clothes like some girl!" my father shouted.

"He's spending it on clothes *because* of some girl!" my mother shouted.

"I don't spend one hundred and fifty dollars on clothes in six months' time," said my father. "You've spent that much in one month!"

"You wear a uniform half the time," I said.

"Buddy, *I* don't even spend that much on clothes in six months," said my mother.

I wiped my face with a towel and said between my teeth, slowly, "I do not plan to spend one hundred and fifty dollars every month on clothes. I just needed new things, that's all. I can't go everywhere in dumb, stupid jeans, old shirts, patched pants, and dumb, stupid worn-out shoes!"

"It's summer, for God's sake!" said my father.

"Who are you expecting to meet?"

"He's already met her," said my mother.

"She must be some hotsy-totsy phony!" said my father.

"Well it's been nice talking to you, Dad," I said.

"I can't talk to you," he said.

"You've just proven that," I said.

He got up and sighed and stood for a minute with his hands on his hips. He looked miserable, but I didn't help him out any. He'd just had a haircut and he has these big ears, and he had that raw kid's look that was in all the old photographs of the days when he and my mother were first married. Whenever I looked at the family album I felt sorry for my father. He'd be standing in our yard, which didn't have any trees in those days or any grass; he'd be holding this little bundle in his arms with a little head sticking out of it (that was me) and he'd look like he'd sure bitten off more than he could chew. My mother was quite a beauty in those days and she looked sure of herself and up to settling down and being a wife and mother, but there was something about my poor dad that said he should have still been riding bicycles with the boys, or hanging around the pizza parlor making cracks at the girls who went by. He didn't look ready for the Mr. and Mrs. towels my grandmother Boyle had given them for a wedding present.

"I don't know, Buddy," my father said. He ran his palm through his short-cropped hair and shook his head. He never could talk very well about things and he hated it that he sometimes got mad when he was trying to.

"Don't worry," I said. "I'm watching it."

"Yeah," he said, as though he had his doubts.

"I didn't buy me a tuxedo yet," I said. I smiled at him.

He gave me back one of his red-faced, lopsided smiles and said, "That'll be next, a monkey suit. Huh?" He gave me a punch in my gut.

I feinted one near his jaw. "Don't worry," I said. "I won't make your mistake."

"What's my mistake?"

"Getting married before you were dry behind your ears."

"Oh I like that," said my mother. "Thanks a lot for that."

My dad laughed and sniffed and tried to land another one on me. I ducked and said, "Get outta here."

He threw his hands up in the air and muttered something like "oh what the heck," then walked out. So much for our talk.

When he went into the kitchen to get a bottle of

beer, my mother followed him. I could hear them talking in low voices. I suppose she was giving it to him, but not really bad because she was always the first to say Dad had trouble expressing himself.

I went into the bedroom and started looking through all the new stuff I'd bought, while Streaker curled up in the top bunk and pretended to be asleep.

"I know you're awake," I said.

He didn't answer me.

"Maybe Mom should put you to bed every night around seven o'clock," I said. "You obviously get all worn out by this time."

He didn't rise to the bait.

I guess I bought so many clothes because I didn't know very much about clothes. Not *clothes*. I knew about putting on what everybody else puts on to go to school or hang around, but I didn't know what to show up in for my first date with Skye Pennington. I chose a pair of white slacks and a white shirt with this red belt. I had a white cotton jacket to go with it, so I decided to do a white number. My tan was started. I liked white with a tan.

Streaker was pretending to snore.

"Well, little bitsy teeny-tiny kids are always put to sleep by big people's talk," I said. Streaker still didn't bite. He stuck with his act. Once, while I was buttoning my shirt, I whirled around and caught him looking at me through his baby fingers, which he had over his face.

"Caught you!" I laughed, but he wanted more of a game. I wasn't up to it. I was too nervous about my date.

I was always giving myself lectures about being more of a big brother to Streaker. He was too little to tag along with me most places I went. Where we lived there weren't any other kids his age nearby. He spent a lot of his time wandering around to neighbors' houses, like old Mrs. Schneider's up on Underwood Drive, where he always got fed fudge brownies. I'd vow to spend more time with him when I was home, but something always came up. After school was out, I got a job at The Sweet Mouth Soda Shoppe, and shortly after that Skye Pennington came waltzing in with her gang. From that day on my life seemed to have one focus, and I'd go over and over our conversations, sifting through them for meanings that probably weren't there, looks that probably didn't mean anything, whatever I could use to spin a fantasy with.

Then I just came out with it one afternoon. "I'd like to take you out Friday night."

"I'd like to have you take me out Friday night."

That was it.

My mother appeared in the doorway of the bedroom and said, "What are you smiling at?"

"I was remembering something."

"Where's Streaker?"

"He's in a coma up there," I said. "He did a swan dive off the bed and hit his head on the Yahtzee dice. I can't wake him up."

Streaker's little body was choking on suppressed laughter.

"Buddy," my mother said, "it isn't that you're not supposed to date girls who aren't in our class. It's just that if you need to go out and spend a whole year's savings on clothes to date one, she's not worth it."

"I won't know that until the night's over," I said.

"Oh yeah, what could make it worth it, huh? One hundred and fifty dollars. What could make it worth it?"

"Don't ask," I said.

"Buddy, don't get fresh with me." She put on one of her stern looks and folded her arms and stared at me. She always looked older than my dad, but when she put on weight the way she was doing at the beginning of that summer, she really added years to her age. She was forty, but she looked five or six years older.

"I'm not getting fresh," I said.

"It sounded fresh." She has long blond hair which goes all the way to her waist, when it isn't done up on top of her head the way it was that night. She has the bluest eyes of any of us Boyles; we all have blue eyes, and she has the greatest smile. She and Streaker are the smilers in the family.

"I'm sorry if it sounded fresh. I wish everybody wouldn't worry so. I can take care of myself, Mom."

"I know that. Just don't turn into a snob like your grandfather."

I have only one living grandfather and it's her father, but she never calls him her anything; she doesn't even call him Dad or Papa. He lives in Montauk now, which is a twenty-minute drive from Seaville, but she never goes there to see him.

"*Jawohl!*" I said. "*Wie geht's?*" spitting out what little German I knew. My mother was actually born in Germany, but she left before she could walk or talk, and never knew her father. He didn't even look her up until she was a grown woman, never even tried to write her or write to anyone to find out if she and her mother were all right.

By the time he got around to caring about his daughter, it was too late. I think my mother hates him.

"One thing I can't stand is a snob!" my mother said.

"Grandpa Trenker doesn't seem like such a snob." I'd met him only twice, once when I was little, and don't remember; once when my mother took me to see him in Montauk. He lives in this huge house by the ocean. He seemed all right to me, one of these foreign types with the classical music going and a lot of talk about his gardens. I couldn't wait to leave, though, because my mother was so uncomfortable around him. She just thought I ought to meet him, she said; he is your grandfather, she said, and he doesn't have two heads or anything, so you'll see for yourself.

"Grandpa Trenker doesn't think his you-know-what smells," my mother said. She couldn't bring herself to say the word "pee," so she made the expression sound worse than it was.

"Well I'm not going to turn into Grandpa Trenker, so don't worry," I said.

"Streaker," my mother said, "I know you're awake. Get down from there and put on your pajamas."

Streaker didn't move.

"All in white," my mother said, looking me over, smiling. "Streaker! Get down from there this minute and put on your pajamas!"

Streaker sat up and glared down at us. "I'm not

110

going to sleep in those dumb, stupid old pajamas!" he blurted out.

"Little pitchers have big ears," my mother said.

"I'm not!" Streaker said. "I'm not going to wear those dumb, stupid pajamas."

"Good-bye, big shot," I said to him. "Good-bye, Mom. I have to rush."

"All in white," my mom said. "You look like Prince Charming."

"All in white!" Skye Pennington exclaimed when she greeted me. "You look like a waiter."

"The specialty tonight is rack of lamb," I said, swallowing my chagrin and borrowing some lines from my busboy days at Gurney's Inn. "The fish is fluke."

"You're the fluke," she laughed, touching my jacket sleeve with her long fingers, the nails pointed, and painted pink like the soft cardigan she wore over her shoulder. "Don't go away. I want Mom and Daddy to meet you."

She ran off with her long black hair bouncing down her back, and left me standing by the pool. In front of the pool house a trio was playing a squeaky rendition of the old Beatles song "Yesterday." It had never sounded worse. The other guests were milling around in little cliques holding drinks. I turned my back on them and pretended to be absorbed by the fantastic view of the dunes and the ocean, which were about four hundred feet away. I was sure I didn't know anyone there, anyway; most of them were older.

The name of the Pennington estate was Beauregard. We've got some summer neighbors on our street who call their place "God's Little Half Acre." They rent shares in it, and in June, July, and August there are always a half dozen beat-up cars crowding the driveway. There were cars crowding the driveway at Beauregard, too. I'd never seen so many Mercedes in one place in my entire life.

To get to Beauregard, I'd had to thumb three rides, which took me only to the entranceway. Then I'd had to walk about a mile up to the house, if you can call a mansion a house. It came complete with an English butler named Peacock. He didn't come right out and say I looked like a waiter, but before I had a chance to say anything, he asked me if I was from Country Cook, which is a catering service. Then he started to direct me to another entrance.

I remember a story Oliver Kidd told me once about going to dinner in New York City with his uncle. They went to the Plaza Hotel, and Ollie was trying to pretend he always ate in places where there were maître d's hovering around and filet mignon for thirty dollars on the menu. When the waiter asked them what they wanted for dessert, Ollie looked at the list and ordered Assorted Pies.

I had the idea I was probably going to do something like that before the night was over.

Skye seemed to be gone for a long, long time, and I was just beginning to think I couldn't maintain my pose of being this cool character enjoying the ocean view. I was shifting my weight from one foot to the other, shoving my hands in my pocket, taking them out again, licking my lips and combing my hair with my fingers when someone came up to me.

"One fish out of water meets another," he said.

I turned around and looked at him. He had on bright red pants, a red-green-and-white plaid jacket, and a bright green shirt. I'm six foot one and he came up to my shoulder. He was bald, and he wore these yellow-tinted glasses with a hearing aid attached. He was puffing on a fake cigarette, the kind smokers use when they first give up the habit. The cigarette glowed red when he breathed in on it. I figured he was about fifty, and I could smell a sickly sweet cologne or after-shave he had on.

"Oh yeah?" I said, because I couldn't come up with anything to say to the idea he saw himself somehow linked up with me.

"My name's Nick," he said.

I said, "I'm Buddy."

"You don't know anybody here, either, do you, Buddy?"

"I've got a date with Skye Pennington."

He made the cigarette glow. "A blind date?"

"No, not a blind date, either."

"You been dating her long?"

"Not that long." I was beginning to get a little steamed.

"I didn't think so."

"Why didn't you think so?"

He shrugged.

"Well why?" I persisted.

"Do you live out here?"

"Yes."

"Year round?"

"Yes."

"I thought so," he said.

"Why did you think so?"

"You're a townie," he said. "You live in town. That's what we used to call them when I went to college. We called girls we dated who weren't in sororities and lived in town, townies. You're a male townie."

"What's wrong with that?" I asked him.

"I'm not looking for anything wrong," he said.

"I'm looking for explanations, that's all."

"I'm looking for *you*," a voice behind me said, and then Skye grabbed my hand. "Daddy," she said, "this is Buddy."

Yellow glasses moved away and I stared up at this gargantuan man with thick white hair, sea green eyes like Skye's, and a tan that made me look anemic. He got my hand in the vise of his fingers and pumped it hard twice, then dropped it. "I'm glad to know you, Buddy. Mrs. Pennington has an appointment and can't meet you. She sends her apologies."

"Pleased to meet you, sir," I said. I was wondering what kind of an appointment someone could have in the middle of a party, and glad that I remembered the sir. Ollie Kidd always said if you sir'd the girl's father, you were already ahead of the game.

"Daddy, we don't have to stick around here, do we?" Skye asked. Anything bad that had happened to me since I'd arrived at Beauregard was made up for by the way she looked: nearly as tall as I, thin with a full figure most thin girls don't have, Skye was all in pink right down to her sandals; tan legs that were straight and strong looking—that long, shining black hair spilling down her back, her great, white smile. I wanted to grab her hand and run the length of the beach with her, so we'd never meet anyone else or get back for a long time.

"Where do you plan to go?" Mr. Pennington directed the question to me.

Skye answered it. "We're just going to drive around, Daddy, maybe go to some of the hangouts." It was the first mention I heard of driving around and I was about to say that I didn't have a car, when Skye said, "Can we take the Jensen?"

"What are the names of these hangouts?" Mr. Pennington asked.

I hadn't been planning to take her to them, but I answered, "The Surf Club, Dunn's, The Sweet Mouth Soda Shoppe." I'd planned to go to the beach, never figuring the beach was her backyard. The kids all hung around Main Beach, and I knew Ollie'd be there with his car. Maybe we'd get something to eat later at Dunn's.

"Do these hangouts serve liquor?" Mr. Pennington asked.

"Oh Daddy, every place serves liquor. What kind of a question is that?" said Skye. "We serve liquor, too."

"Do you drink, Buddy?" Mr. Pennington asked me.

"No, sir, I don't."

"Do you drive?"

"I have a license," I said, but I didn't say I was sixteen and couldn't drive after nine, and didn't have a car anyway. It was my first realization that I was younger than Skye.

Mr. Pennington said, "You can take the Jensen if Skye drives. You're to be back here at midnight, Skye."

"Will I turn into a pumpkin if I'm not?" She laughed.

"Do you understand, Buddy?" Mr. Pennington asked me.

"Yes, sir," I said.

Then he reached down and put his long arms around her and hugged her very hard, as though she was taking off on a cross-country tour.

"Be careful, baby," I heard him whisper. "I love you."

I didn't meet anyone else at Beauregard that night. Skye took my hand and led me through the crowd, chattering all the way.

"Mummy's appointment is with her spiritualist, could you die?"

"Really?"

"Yes, really. His name is Bachoo and he's into astral travel and everything and Mummy would leave an audience with the Pope if he showed up,

117

which he just did. Daddy says he always shows up just when Daddy's flown in Dungeness crabmeat from the coast, which Daddy just did for this party, and there won't be any left, either, because Bachoo's The Human Hoover—that's Daddy's name for him—he just breathes in food like a vacuum cleaner sucking up dust."

Just at that point in her rambling, we passed the red pants and the plaid jacket in a cloud of that sickly sweet scent, with his yellow glasses turned toward me. "G'night, Buddy," he called after me.

"Good night," I said.

"Do you know Mr. De Lucca?" Skye asked me.

"I just met him."

"He's the token writer tonight," Skye said. "Mummy found everybody but a black. A writer, a couple of artists, this divine astrologist, and even a man who plays the bagpipes. We're lucky we don't have to be here for that. He plays 'Amazing Grace' off-key, and it's just hairy to hear, I promise you!"

"That guy's a writer?" I said. "That guy in the yellow glasses?"

"His name's Nick De Lucca," Skye said.

"What's he written?"

"He's a journalist," Skye said. "Mummy found him through Bachoo. He did a story on spirituality in the Hamptons or some darn thing. Hey, the garage is this way." She pulled me down a stone walk away from the house and then let go of my hand, as though now that we were alone it wasn't right to hold hands. Maybe she was just shy when she wasn't around a lot of people, I figured, because she stopped chattering, too. We walked along in the moonlight, silently, for a while. Behind us, I could hear the trio playing "Shine On, Harvest Moon."

"I've never been in a Jensen," I said, and immediately wished I hadn't said it. I'd never even heard of a Jensen, but I'd planned to play it cooler before I just blurted that out.

"That's all right," she said. "Most people haven't. It isn't your ordinary, everyday car." She fumbled in her bag for the keys while we walked toward a large, barnlike building. "Oh here're my keys," she said. "Are you happy, Buddy?" She stopped then and looked at me, taking me completely by surprise.

"Sure I'm happy," I said, sounding like some slow-wit.

She looked at me for a moment, her eyes fixing right on mine, and I looked away, because it was too much. She was too much; the whole thing was, and I was beginning to think I wasn't enough.

She walked up very close to me and said very solemnly, "I want you to be happy with me, Buddy."

"Okay," I managed. I croaked it out actually. I

didn't understand her, or I wasn't up to her, or ready for her, but I wanted to be. Oh how I wanted to be.

Then she did what I thought she was going to do and told myself of course she wasn't going to do that—she put her hands very gently on my face a second, looked into my eyes, and I felt her soft, moist mouth just for the sweetest, shortest time press against my mouth.

I didn't touch her, and before I had a chance to say anything she smiled, stepped away, touched something I didn't see, and the garage door opened, lights went on to display six sleek cars, one a Rolls. She moved toward the last one on the left, dark green. "The Jenny," she said. "Want a lift somewhere, sailor?"

I wondered if I'd ever be able to talk again, or walk without my knees trembling, or breathe without my heart slamming into my ribs. But I got in beside her, and when she asked me while she was backing out where I wanted to go—"Make it someplace special, Buddy"—I heard myself answering in a very confident tone, "Montauk."

"What's there?" she said.

"My grandfather," I told her. Just like that, it came out of my mouth, and Skye let out a laugh that was like a whoop, and said, "Oh Buddy, that's subtle! I'm going to like you, Buddy Boyle, I can tell."

✳

"Hello, Grandpa? This is Buddy." There was a long pause. Skye was parked at the corner waiting for me while I phoned him. I could see some guys walking back and forth admiring the Jensen, or admiring Skye, and Skye smiling at them. Why did she have to smile at them, I thought, and my stomach tightened; it would tighten all summer over any little thing like that, anyone coming near her.

"Buddy?" My grandfather finally spoke. "Ingeborg's boy?"

"Yes," I said. "I'm in Montauk."

"Is anything wrong?"

"Nothing's wrong," I said. "I'm just in Montauk."

"I see. I——" I couldn't blame him for not being able to think of anything to say. Our family had been about as interested in Grandpa Trenker since he'd moved to Montauk ten years ago as we were interested in Rumanian Gypsies or gamma rays.

"I suppose it's a lousy time to pay a visit," I said.

"Not at all," he said. "Is that what you want to do?"

"I have a girl with me," I said.

"How fortunate for you," he said. "Do you know the directions?"

He gave them to me, and warned me that at the end of his private driveway there'd be a chain across the road with a padlock attached to it.

"It isn't locked," he said. "Just undo it, then drive all the way to the end. I'll put on lights for you. You'll hear Mignon barking."

"Does he bite?" I said.

"She," he said. "No, she won't bite you. Are you coming right now?"

"Right now, if that's okay."

He said it was, and I ran from the phone booth to the Jensen. All the guys who'd been shuffling around the car stood there gaping at us as we took off, and I thought of how many times I'd been the gaper. Then I watched Skye's profile while she drove up Old Montauk Highway, and felt the chill as we neared the ocean, and smelled the salt spray. It was like a dream, I thought, and I wondered if it would always seem like a dream and never seem natural to be with her.

You couldn't see my grandfather's house from the road. There were woods all around, and after I undid the chain, we started up the long hill. His house sat right on the edge of a cliff overlooking the ocean. The first time I'd ever seen it—the only time—it hadn't been dark as it was that night, and all I could think of as I stared at it, formidable and superb standing there in the sun with the blue ocean stretched out beyond it, was that nobody related to me could live in that house.

"Nice" was what Skye said at our first glimpse of the place.

Grandpa Trenker had the yard bathed in light.

"Oh, and who's *he*?" Skye squealed as she got out and this shaggy dog came running to greet us.

"It's a she," I said. "Her name's Mignon."

"Hello, Mignon," Skye said, letting the dog jump up on her and lick her arm. "What kind of a dog are you? Are you an opera and not a dog, because I know an opera named *Mignon*, but I've never seen a dog like you!"

"She's both an opera and a dog"—my grandfather's voice—and he stepped out of the shadows then, walking toward Skye with his hand extended.

Skye took his hand. "I've never *seen* a dog like this!" she squealed again, and Mignon kept jumping on her. "What *kind* of a dog is this? I thought I knew every kind of dog there is! My mother, Mummy, used to raise green-eyed, all-white Pomeranians, which are kind of rare—but what are you, honey?" Skye said to the dog. I was beginning to realize she chattered very fast when she was nervous.

"Down, Mignon!" my grandfather said sharply. The dog obeyed instantly.

"Mignon is a keeshond," said my grandfather. "And I'm Frank Trenker."

"I'm Skye Pennington. How do you do, Mr. Trenker."

"Hello, Grandpa," I said.

"Good evening, Buddy."

"A keeshond," Skye babbled on as we walked toward the house. "I've never heard of a keeshond and I've been dragged to dog shows since I was old enough to toddle, believe me. I thought I'd seen every breed there was, but a keeshond, oh Mignon, aren't you special, and I LOVE *Mignon*, the opera, too. 'Adieu, *Mignon*,' " she sang, and my grandfather chuckled. They walked ahead of me.

My grandfather might be a snob, I thought, but he has something to be a snob about. Did you ever see the old, spooky movies on TV with Boris Karloff in them? He's this very tall, thin, very undaunted character, thick white hair, a mustache—my grandfather looks something like him, only he's not spooky. He's dignified, and confident, and you just know that in his day he was really something else, and he's still an extraordinarily handsome man. I'd turn around on the street to get another look at him, even if he wasn't my grandfather. He's that kind of man. You notice him; you know he's special in some way. He's in his sixties, but he's one of those men who you don't think of as an old man. When I went to Montauk to see him that time with my mother, I thought all those same things about him, but I was trying to see him through my mother's eyes, and I didn't let myself admire him. I tried to imagine how I'd feel if my dad just ducked out on me while I was growing up, and then reappeared and tried to say he was my father. I'd have had the same reaction, I guess: you can just take that father bit and stuff it!

But he hadn't done anything to *me*, had he? At some point bygones had to be bygones, and I guess we were at that point that night. I was, anyway.

My grandfather had this opera going on the stereo when we walked inside the house, and Skye gave another squeal and said it was her favorite aria of all, and she sang *"Un—bel—di,"* and did a little spin and clapped her hands. *"Madame Butterfly!"* she said.

She said to me, "Butterfly is singing 'One fine day,' Buddy. She's saying one day there'll be a thread of smoke rising from the ocean, and her husband's ship will come into the harbor, and he'll rush up to the little house on the hilltop to greet her."

"Very good," my grandfather said.

I didn't say anything, but I'd noticed that Skye realized I didn't know one opera from another, which didn't make me feel great even though it was true. About the only serious music we ever played in our house was Perry Como's version of "The Lord's Prayer."

My grandfather's house was filled with books and paintings and the kind of furniture my mother called "fancy antique stuff." Skye waltzed around admiring everything, and I remembered when I visited there with my mother, the thing that impressed me the most was the view of the ocean from the windows. Skye saw that view all the time at Beauregard. We couldn't see it very well in the dark, anyway, but we could hear the waves crashing down on the beach, and we could see the lights of the other houses arcing down the coastline.

There was a glass of wine on the table beside a large leather chair. In front of the chair, on the oriental rug, there was a bag of sunflower seeds. My grandfather explained he was just about to fill his bird feeders.

"The birds like to feed early in the morning," he said, "before I'm up. I'm a night owl, so I fill the feeders before I go to bed."

"Oh, you'd love Mummy, my mother," Skye said, "she's a bird lover, too, and she keeps track of every bird she's ever seen, about one hundred and fifty varieties, and when I was a kid she'd drag me out here to the walking dunes at Oysters Pond to spot birds. I mean, what did *I* care about birds, but now I wish I'd paid attention because I don't know an oriole from a robin."

"It's never too late to learn," said my grandfather.

"I'd really like to learn," Skye said. "I really admire birds, they're so *free*. I mean, they *symbolize* freedom."

"Far from it," said my grandfather.

Skye said, *"What?"*

"I said far from it. Birds look free but they're not, you know. They're very restricted. They're prisoners, really, of their own territory. They can't move easily from one territory to another."

Skye looked at him a moment, eye to eye, carefully, the way she'd looked at me in the driveway at Beauregard when she told me she wanted me to be happy with her. Then she said, "I really admire you, Mr. Trenker. You're subtle. I mean, you're really subtle—and I like all of this—" her arms sweeping out to indicate the whole room, everything. "I do."

When Skye called something or someone subtle,

it was her highest compliment, I gathered. I just sat on the couch and let them talk, congratulating myself for bringing her there. I remembered an English teacher we had once describing something called "borrowed glory" to us. Borrowed glory was when you couldn't think of a way to say something, so you got out Bartlett's *Familiar Quotations*, looked up "love" or "fear" or "patriotism"—whatever subject you had on your mind—and you copied down what Shakespeare or Emerson or someone famous had said about it, and put that into your composition as a quote. This teacher used to say just because you could find a quote about something didn't mean you'd really expressed *yourself*. It just meant you'd borrowed glory. He said there were all sorts of ways to borrow glory. If your family was rich and you were conceited about it—that was borrowing glory, too, because you hadn't done anything to make them rich—you were just coasting on their abilities.

So that night I was borrowing glory by letting my grandfather make the impression on Skye Pennington, instead of trying to impress her with my own personality.

Well, thank God for borrowed glory, I thought. Thank God I had someone in my family to borrow it from, because all the while I sat there watching

Skye, I told myself I wasn't going to let her slip through my fingers. Whatever it took to keep her in my life, I was going to do it . . . even if it meant learning about opera, which had always sounded to me like a lot of people screeching around in German or Italian with music drowning them out until they could get their breaths again.

We spent a lot of that evening—or they did— talking about animals. My grandfather was this great animal lover. He had a whole pot of plain spaghetti cooked which he put out on his back patio for raccoons to have. He had a light fixed so we could see them sneaking in from the woods, one by one, taking the spaghetti in their little hands and winding it all around themselves while they sucked it into their mouths. They looked like little masked bandits, and a few of them stretched out on their backs like clowns and fed the spaghetti into their mouths in long strings. They took marshmallows from his hand, and he let Skye feed a few to them, and she looked over her shoulder at me with this expression of sheer joy on her face, as though she'd never done anything so fantastic in all her life.

About eleven o'clock I said we'd better leave, remembering Mr. Pennington's order that Skye was to be home by midnight. Skye got up and went into the bathroom, leaving me with my grandfather, the first time in my life I'd ever been alone with him. I couldn't think of anything to say, and we just sat there for a moment while he took a sip of his wine and looked across at me.

"Do you think you impressed her, Buddy?" he finally said.

"Well, *you* did," I mumbled, and his remark had made my face red.

He didn't say anything, so I said, "It was borrowed glory, I guess."

"I'm happy to lend it to you," he said.

"Thanks."

"How is your mother?"

"She's fine," I said. "We're all fine."

I was hoping he wasn't going to try and make some excuse about what he did to my mother, what he didn't do for her, or try to explain it, and I needn't have worried. He didn't mention her again. He sat there sipping his wine while I drank what was left of my ginger ale and wondered how anyone could stand opera—there was another one playing, some woman shrieking, then a man bellowing some sort of answer.

"You know, Buddy," my grandfather finally said, "you can get there on your own, once you're pointed in the right direction."

"Get where?" I said, but I knew what he was

talking about. He knew I knew, too, and didn't even bother explaining where.

"I'd be happy to point you, if that's what you want," he said.

"What do you think of her?" I said.

"She's very beautiful," he answered. *"Very."*

"But beauty's only skin deep, huh?" I said. "That's something my mother is always saying."

"On the contrary," he said. " 'Spend all you have for loveliness,/Buy it, and never count the cost;/For one white singing hour of peace/Count many a year of strife well lost./And for a breath of ecstasy/Give all you have been or could be.' "

Somebody spouting off poetry always made me a little self-conscious, unless it was a teacher who had to for a class assignment or something. I couldn't think of anything to say.

"One of your American poets wrote that," said my grandfather. "Sara Teasdale."

"What you're telling me is she's worth it, even if I do have to bring her out here to impress her."

"What I'm telling you," he said, "is that *you're* worth it, too, that with a little polish, you won't have to bring her out here, although she's always welcome."

"I haven't even been out of Seaville," I said, "except to go to Disneyland once with my folks . . .

and Block Island another time with my dad."

My grandfather smiled. "It isn't where you've been," he said. "An ass who goes traveling doesn't come back a horse."

"She's also older than I am," I said. "I don't know how much older, but she is."

"A woman you love is always older than you are, even when she's younger."

"I don't know what that means," I said.

"When you love a woman, she seems secret and mysterious," said my grandfather, "things you associate with the full bloom instead of the bud."

"She's rich, too," I said. "The Penningtons have tons of money."

"Obstacles are challenges for winners, and excuses for losers," said my grandfather.

"I never thought of it that way," I said.

Skye came back from the bathroom then, and my grandfather walked us down to her car.

"I hope I see you again, Mr. Trenker," said Skye. "This has been such a super evening, and Mummy's not going to believe a raccoon ate out of my hand. I don't even believe it myself. I can't wait to spring keeshond on her, too. She'll die if she's never heard of one, you know, it's like telling the Pope he doesn't know all his cardinals or something."

"Come again," my grandfather said, looking

straight at me, "if you want to."

"If we *want* to!" Skye exclaimed. "Does a starling want one of your sunflower seeds!"

"Not very much," said my grandfather. "He has trouble getting the shells open."

"The one time I wanted to show off and say a starling or a blue jay or something besides just a plain bird, I pick the wrong bird." Skye laughed. "I like you so much, Mr. Trenker. You're subtle!"

"I try to be," my grandfather said.

All the way back to Beauregard, Skye did seventy, talking nonstop about him.

"You don't mind going fast, do you, Buddy?" she asked me.

"It doesn't feel like we're going too fast," I told her, but it did, and we were, and I knew I wasn't going to do anything to stop it.

⁓ 2 ⁓

A

Firecracker Explodes

I Stay Near You

You're lucky if you move next door to an idea, as I did that summer *Gentlehands* came to me. I wrote the book in six weeks without pause. It flowed from my typewriter as though a tape were inside the machine. It was the only book of mine that required no rewrite. It was published "as is."

But more often a writer racks her brain for a good story, sifts through all of her experiences, and very often imagines she is out of ideas. Blocked.

Paul Zindel spoke of this at a school where we were both appearing one day. I was to follow him, a particular pleasure for me—not following him (I dreaded that) but being on the same program with him. He is one of the reasons I began writing for young adults. I'd been primarily a mystery/suspense writer, but once I read *The Pigman*, I was inspired to try to write something in this genre.

As I listened to Paul describe the frustrations of trying to get a good idea, I felt some gratification knowing that someone as capable as Paul went through the same thing I did. He gave a perfect picture of the ordeal, and I sat in the audience nodding my head in agreement. Then suddenly: *BANG!* Everyone jumped! What was *that*? A sneak move. Paul had exploded a firecracker. He was dramatizing the way, finally, an idea comes—*BOOM!*—there it is!

That happened to me one night at a huge banquet for librarians in a midwestern city. I was to give a workshop at a school the following morning. I was between books, struggling to decide what I would write next, and in a bad mood because I felt as though NO IDEA were written across my forehead.

There were some nine hundred people present, table after table of us in this enormous auditorium. As we were beginning to eat our fruit cups, a huge harp was rolled out on the stage, and a woman in a long red gown sat down beside it and began to play.

It always takes a minute to recognize the melody coming from a harp, but this night there was no way to know what song it was. Not the first piece, not the second, not any tune she strummed. Everyone was talking.

There were people at the dinner who hadn't seen each other in a long time, and there were others making acquaintances. No one was even trying to hear the harpist.

She played on through the dinner, her face quite placid, her hands proficient on the strings of her instrument.

I remarked to someone, "The poor harpist! No one's listening to her."

"She's used to it," I was told. "She plays for these conventions all the time."

After we had lingered over coffee at the end of the meal, I was leaving the auditorium when I glanced at an exit and saw the woman in red waiting while some workers wheeled her harp into the back of a station wagon.

That was when I heard the firecracker.

That was the moment I saw her as a young girl taking her first harp lessons. Suddenly I remembered a girl I'd gone to high school with whose father ran a laundry. Although she had no wish to play the accordion, a neighbor made a deal with her father: She would give accordion lessons to Helen in exchange for free laundry service.

Helen hated the accordion and the fact that she was made to play it at school assemblies with all the kids squirming in their seats, nudging each other, and talking while she struggled through clumsy versions of "Santa Lucia" and "The Beer Barrel Polka."

What follows is from my novel *I Stay Near You*, a firecracker idea that I was already outlining in my notebook before I went to sleep that night.

This three-generational story begins with the teenage harpist, Mildred, as she meets the boy who will change her life irrevocably. At the end of the book she is a grandmother, playing her harp at conventions where nobody listens.

Although the harpist who performed at that banquet will never know it, someone *was* paying attention to her, and this is the result.

❖ I Stay ❖
Near You

I never knew anyone who hated rich people as much as Mildred Cone did.

I first got to know Mildred sophomore year, when she transferred to East High. We sometimes walked home together, down Osborne Street and across Alden Avenue, headed toward the west end.

I didn't live in the west end. My mother didn't like the fact we lived as close to it as we did. It was where the train tracks were; it was near the dump, and The Cayuta Rope Factory.

Mildred was the only girl in East High School who did live there.

"How come there're no other girls from the west end?" I asked Mildred once.

"There's none of them wants to better themselves," she said.

Mildred's grammar was poor. "Poor" was a word you were never surprised to hear said in the same sentence with Mildred Cone. Her family was poor. She looked poor. We'd say "poor Mildred" when we talked about her.

"I feel so awful," someone in our crowd would say, "because poor Mildred Cone asked me what we were all going to do Friday night, and I lied. Said we weren't doing anything, just staying in."

"I thought I'd never get away from poor Mildred Cone"—someone else—"and I had the feeling she was *this close* to asking if she could eat lunch with us."

"Guess who's playing for tomorrow's assembly?"—another of us. "Poor Mildred Cone, on her harp!"

Besides being an all-around poor thing, Mildred's other big difference from all of us was that she played the harp.

You can imagine how much a bunch of high school kids wants to hear a harp playing in assembly.

Sometimes Mr. Timmerman, the principal, had

to get on his feet and shush us right in the middle of one of Mildred's renditions of "Clair de Lune" or Hungarian Rhapsody No. 2.

I'd asked her about playing the harp during one of those long walks home from school.

Mildred was this gawky fifteen-year-old, so skinny her arms and legs looked like cut-off clothesline poles. She had a bad permanent so her black hair was frizzy. There was nothing starting to show in the bosom department, even though her sweaters were sizes too small, hand-me-downs from an older, married sister.

She had only two sweaters: a red one and a powder-blue one, old as the hills both of them, the kind she always had to pull down over and over, they were so small and shrunken.

She had these big round brown eyes in this pale white face. She didn't look up a lot, or meet your eyes too often. She looked scared. That was her look.

I was no beauty, but I could pass. I was in the crowd. We'd all gone to the same schools together since kindergarten. I was Mildred's age, but blond, with straight hair that fell to my shoulders, the owner of eight sweaters and two A-cup bras.

"Mildred?" I asked her once as we walked along.

"How come you chose the harp to play? Harps are so enormous!"

"There's a harp teacher lives next to us is why," Mildred answered. "She gave me a harp, and I get all my lessons free because my daddy sees she gets her laundry done for nothing."

The Cones didn't own The White Lamb Laundry, but they all worked there. They lived in a house out back. After school and weekends, Mildred waited on customers.

"You play the harp real well," I told her. "I don't mean to say you don't."

"You don't even listen to me play that thing," she said. "No one does."

"A harp is hard to listen to, Mildred. A harp—"

She waved away my attempts at an apology. "I'm going to get me a music scholarship to some college," she said. "That's why I transferred to East High in the first place."

Mildred was one of those all-A students, the type whose hand shot up before a teacher finished asking a question.

English was the only subject she had trouble with, but still she'd get an A−, never go down to B, because she read and understood everything and always memorized double the amount of poetry assigned.

Sometimes when we were walking along like that, the Storms' limousine would pass, on its way across Alden Avenue, and up Fire Hill, to Cake, the Storm estate.

The Storms owned The Cayuta Rope Factory, which had just been made a defense plant because of World War II. It was always the biggest industry in our small town, anyway, and the Storms were the richest people in the entire county.

Cake was the biggest house in the whole county, too. Sitting high above the town, on the top of Fire Hill, it *looked* like a Cake—a huge, white, three-layer one.

Whenever the Cake limousine roared by us, Mildred would snarl, "There they go!"

You never got more than a glimpse of them, the way someone in London, England, might catch a glimpse of the royal family on their way to and from Buckingham Palace.

"Par-don us for liv-ving!" Mildred would continue, as she watched the long, black Packard disappear around the bend.

"Hoity-toity!" Mildred would grumble.

One day I asked her why they made her so mad.

"Who do they think they are?" she answered my question with that one.

"They know who they are. They're the Storms. Period."

"They think their own pee doesn't smell."

"They might be nice. You don't know."

"Nice," she said bitterly.

"You don't know."

"They think they're God's gift to the universe!"

"I saw the son once. Powell Storm, Jr.?"

"Powell!" Mildred spat out his name. "What kind of a first name is Powell supposed to be?"

"He's such a doll, though. He looks like Tyrone Power, the movie star, exactly!"

"I hate rich people!" Mildred said. "You should only know what we find in their pants' pockets sometimes!"

"What do you find?" I imagined far worse than what Mildred had to tell me.

"Fifty-dollar bills sometimes, crumpled up like paper wads. Once a genuine hundred-dollar bill!" Mildred pronounced it "gen-u-wine," and spoke the words in hushed, conspiratorial tones. "It was the first one of them things I ever saw! . . . One time we found a solid-gold watch in a sweater pocket, just as shiny, running good and everything!"

"Do you get to keep what you find?" I asked.

"Keep what we find?" She was outraged. "No, we don't keep what we find! We're not thieves like them! My daddy says the rich get richer and the poor get poorer, because the rich would steal your eyeballs while you're sleeping!"

"Oh, Mildred."

"Don't 'oh Mildred' me, Laura Stewart! You don't go through their clothes! You don't know what they're like! Forget enough money in their pants pockets to feed a whole family for a week!"

I shut up at that point.

"Rich people don't care what they do!" Mildred couldn't stop. "A big old Cadillac ran over our pet bulldog right in back of our house, never stopped, never got out and come in to tell us. He was just this puppy squealing in pain, and all they done was to slow up, look, then speed away. They crushed his leg and he had to have it amputated. . . . I hate them all! They treat you like dirt when you wait on them!"

We might have thought of her as "poor Mildred," but she had a temper that made me back off and give her lots of room. Those big, round, brown eyes would narrow, and she'd thrust her jaw forward, and her hands would ball into tight little fists whenever we got on *that* subject.

It was *that* subject I always remembered most

when I thought back on my conversations with Mildred.

It was *that* subject, and that particular conversation, that would come back to my mind one day when Mildred would tell me: "Laura? I know the telephone number for Cake by heart now."

Junior year someone in our crowd got a new 1943 Ford V-8. After school we'd pile into it and head for Bannon's, the hangout.

I saw Mildred around, but I didn't really see her. I realized that on a Friday morning, near the end of May.

Mildred's enormous heart-shaped gold harp was in place up on the stage of the auditorium. Mr. Timmerman was announcing the names of senior boys who'd miss graduation because they'd enlisted. Mildred would go on next. We were all shifting in our seats, grumbling among ourselves about having to hear her play the stupid harp again, and someone in our row was passing out jawbreakers from a cellophane package.

I popped a green one into my mouth, slid way down in my seat, prepared for the worst, when Mildred walked out from behind the curtain.

I remember the day Alan Fonderosa came to school wearing glasses, and the month Tub

Goldman started dropping weight, and when Fern Aldrich got braces, but the change in Mildred Cone sneaked up on me.

Was it her hair? It couldn't be just her hair.

While Mildred crossed the stage to her harp, the boy beside me nudged my arm with his elbow and sucked in his breath.

"Is it her hair?" I asked him.

"Whatever it is, it's all right with me."

Start with her hair. All the frizz was gone. Her hair was long and soft-looking, shining like coal, falling past her shoulders.

She had on a black peasant skirt, with a very low-cut white peasant blouse, and this fake white gardenia pinned in her hair. Yes, all that was new.

But when had she grown the large breasts, the long, slender legs? She had on a pair of black espadrilles with white rope soles, and black laces that tied around these very slim ankles.

A boy in front of me let out a long wolf whistle— you could see Mildred blush, see a slanted smile flicker and fade, as she stood beside the heart-shaped instrument that towered over her.

"How could someone change overnight like that?" I whispered to the girl on my other side.

"The caterpillar's become a butterfly," she said.

Mildred was going to say something.

That was new, too. She'd never spoken a word before onstage.

I remembered when I used to have trouble hearing Mildred, used to ask her to speak up (unless she was mad about something), but her words were clear, and her manner was sure. She even managed another smile.

"It's my birthday today, so I'd like to play a new song that I learned." She cast a furtive glance at Mr. Timmerman, adding, "It's not classical, if that's okay." And he nodded. "It's popular."

Then Mildred drew a chair under her, pulled the golden harp gently back on her shoulder, and placed her hands on the strings.

It takes a while to figure out what song is playing, when it's played on a harp.

I sat there, waiting for it to register, wondering why I hadn't seen this miraculous change in Mildred. I kept thinking: She's turned beautiful, as though that could happen in a short amount of time, the way a body turned red in the sun, all in an afternoon.

Her hands moved along the strings, and gradually the song began to form, and I knew it. We all did. It was just getting popular. I hadn't bought the record for my collection yet, but I'd planned to.

I had the craziest dream
Last night, yes I did!
I never dreamt it could be,
But there you were, in love with me. . . .

I think we were all saying the words to the song
in our heads, while she let her fingers strum the
wires and Mr. Timmerman nodded his head con-
tentedly.

All I could do was wonder what had brought
about this gigantic change in Mildred Cone, and
who was there in her life she imagined herself having this crazy dream over?

She only played that one number that assembly.

At noon, in the lunchroom, Mildred was *the* subject of conversation. I was not the only one who
hadn't seen the change in Mildred coming; most of
us hadn't. No one had any answers, just questions.
We all watched the boys hanging, like flies around
the sweets, in front of Mildred's table. She was
grinning down at her sandwich, tossing her hair
back the times she glanced up at them. Things were
changing for Mildred.

Days her father brought her harp to school for an
assembly, he used to have to scout down the janitor
for help getting it off and on the laundry truck. . . .
But that May afternoon, I saw the same boys who'd

hung around her at lunch helping Mr. Cone hoist the harp in its huge case up into the back of the truck.

School was almost out before I got to walk our old route home again with Mildred. A day had come when the car I always rode in had broken down, and the boys who always tagged after Mildred had fallen behind us. We were alone together, finally.

The fake gardenia was a regular part of her out-fits by then. She had on one of her tight sweaters, really really tight, and I had the feeling that even if someone were to give Mildred a new, loose sloppy Joe, she'd prefer to stick out all over the place. If it wasn't a tight sweater showing her off, it was a blouse buttoned only halfway up.

Mildred had developed a certain walk that I'd never noticed before, too. It was a kind of a little strut, head back, shoulders back (the way my mother said mine should go: Watch your *pos*-ture, Laura!). And that hair of hers. Mildred had worked up a little routine. First she'd look out at you from behind the hair, then she'd give it a toss back and look directly into your eyes . . . then it'd fall back, she'd look out at you almost timidly, then whamo, tossed back, eyes fixed on yours. I can see how it'd make boys' knees turn to jelly, and I even tried to

149

imitate it myself a few times in front of the bath-room mirror . . . but it was Mildred's gesture. No one could make it quite the way she could.

That afternoon I said, "I loved that song you played in assembly the other day."

"You didn't even listen." She gave her same old answer, but this time, almost as though she knew she couldn't get away with it, she added, "Did you? I picked out a popular song purposely so people would listen."

"Oh, we listened," I said. "Are you in love with someone or what?"

"Or what," she said flatly. She always did have a mouth on her.

"Well, you seem so changed, that's why I asked."

"My music teacher's coaching me in stage pres-ence. I'm developing a stage presence. I want to get into Juilliard."

"You're developing more than a stage presence," I said slyly, but Mildred looked at me, and past me, as though she hadn't heard me, or had heard me and didn't know what I was talking about. Those were the only two possibilities I could come up with right then. I still didn't really know Mildred.

"Miss Laurel—that's my music teacher—Miss Laurel says I have a good chance of getting a schol-arship."

The old Mildred would have said "getting me a scholarship."

"I hope you get one. I don't know what I want to do, now that there's a war."

"War or no war: I just want to get out of this town, and be somebody!"

"I like Cayuta, though."

"You're not stuck here, Laura, that's why."

"I'm as stuck here as you are."

"So far. But your daddy can afford to send you to college."

"He says he won't if my grades don't improve. Says it'd just be a waste of money."

We were walking along like that, with me pondering this new way of Mildred's, an almost serene side I'd never seen, serene but calculating, thinking ahead, when suddenly one of the cars from Cake came careening by, going sixty, seventy, way past the speed limit.

You could always tell cars from Cake by the license plates. This was some kind of sports car, with CAKE 2 on the plate.

"There they go!" I said what she always said.

"They've got some nerve!" The old sound of Mildred Cone came back.

No matter that there was only one person in the car from Cake, we always said "they."

Mildred said between her teeth, "I hope they wrap themselves around a tree!"

That was one way Mildred Cone hadn't changed, and I gave a little laugh, teasing, "They still get under your skin, don't they, Mil."

I don't know where the "Mil" had come from. I guess my mind had decided that this new Mildred deserved a new name.

"*Mildred*," she was quick to correct me. "I don't like my name shortened."

Then she went back to the Storms. "Who do they think they are?"

It was the old familiar question.

It wasn't many weeks before Mildred Cone would have a real, first-hand answer.

Naturally, the Cone family didn't belong to The Cayuta Yacht Club, but the summer of '43 Mildred spent her days at C.Y.C.

Waitresses had replaced bar boys carrying drinks to people out on the lawn. Any boy in Cayuta could find a job for more money, because so many of the young men were going into the service.

Everybody had a job that summer. It was unpatriotic to do nothing at all. I worked four afternoons a week in my father's insurance office. One of his regular girls had gone to work in a defense factory.

Fridays I'd spend the whole day at the yacht club.

I'd take my knitting for when I wasn't out in my Comet sailboat. A lot of us girls would knit on the lawn in the late afternoon, waiting to see what boys would come for swims after work, or go out for sunset sails.

Hands down, Powell Storm, Jr., was the one we all said could put his shoes under our beds any day. None of us had ever been to bed with a boy, but we always said things like that. When a real sharp boy passed by, one of us would say, so the others could hear but he couldn't, "Oh, take me, darlin'. I'm yours if you want me." We'd say, "I surrender, dear," and "I should have known you were temptation."

We'd get all that from songs, and we'd toss off these lines while we knitted one and purled two, never dreaming we weren't the most sophisticated girls anywhere in the world.

Some of us had started smoking, and we'd follow a good line with a long stream of smoke, sometimes let out through our noses. A few of us could blow smoke rings.

I remember that certain Friday in late June very clearly, because it was the first time I ever saw all the Storms up close. There was the old grandmother, the mother, the father, the daughter named Pesh, then Powell.

They'd all come in from sailing on their boat—the biggest boat on the lake, with both sails and a motor. They were having afternoon cocktails at a redwood table on the long, green lawn that spread down to the lake water. It was a picture-postcard afternoon—that's how my mother'd describe it. She'd say, "This is pretty enough to be a postcard," when she saw beautiful scenery, as though postcards were lovelier than life.

Even my own mother would have stared at the Storms, same as we were all doing. I don't know who in Cayuta could have resisted it. Oh, there were some who could have, but they were the ones we would have stared at if the Storms weren't living in our town. They were the next-to-richest, who owned smaller businesses than P. T. Storm's rope factory, but bigger ones than Schmidt's Department Store or Lattimore's Ford Motors.

"Powell Storm, Jr.," Babs Check said, "you can just roll me right over in the clover." Babs was lighting up a Chesterfield stuck in a long, ivory holder. She was the oldest of us, seventeen, owner of the Ford. She was the only one who didn't look around when she lit up, to be sure no one who knew her family was watching. She had permission to smoke.

"Ravish me, ravish me, ravish me," said Molly

Parker to Powell's profile down the lawn.

I said, "Violate me in the violet time, in the vilest way that you know."

Then Babs let some smoke out of her mouth, made it curl up into her nose (the only one in the crowd who could get smoke to do that), and she said, "Well. Look who's sashaying down their way with a whole trayful of Tom Collinses."

"Mildred Cone," I said. "Dear old Mildred."

Mildred's uniform was a white middy blouse and navy skirt with a red silk neckerchief. Her long hair was tied back with a red ribbon.

"Boy, do I wish I had her hair!" Babs said.

"Or her boobs," Molly said.

"Or her legs," Babs said.

"Who wants her harp?" I said.

"Oh, don't re-mind us!" Babs howled.

Powell didn't even look up at Mildred. His sister gave Mildred a fast glance, a one-second acknowledgment that something was being put on the table. (Pesh Storm was older than Powell. She was already in her last year at Wellesley College.) Mother, father, and grandmother probably couldn't have told you if a male or female had set down their frosty drinks with the maraschino cherries floating in them.

Powell was tipped back in a captain's chair, legs

155

stretched out, tanned, wearing white short shorts so short you'd swear any minute you'd see all of him. He was staring out at the sailboats coming and going on the lake, almost as though he wasn't with his family. He had dark, brooding looks. He looked like what you'd think Heathcliff looked like in *Wuthering Heights*, half savage, half gentleman, and he looked like the movie star Tyrone Power exactly. He had on a white shirt, unbuttoned all the way down, eyes so bright blue you could see their color clear across the lawn.

"He's got such a hairy chest!" Molly said.

"I bet he's real hairy *all* over!" Babs said.

"That's all right, Ape Man," I said, "crush my bones." In a while Mildred came sauntering toward us, carrying the empty tray, slowing up some while we all said hi, stopping by me a second to whisper: "To *what* do we owe this big honor, I wonder?" snidely, bobbing her head in the Storms' direction.

"Do you shampoo with Halo?" Babs asked her. "Is that what makes your hair shine?"

"I rinse with beer. That's the secret."

"Beer?" We'd none of us heard that one before.

"My married sister gave me that tip," Mildred said.

"How come you don't smell beery?" Molly asked.

156

"You just don't. . . . I don't, do I?"

We were just talking away, and over by the barbecue pit the accordionist was strapping on her instrument. She played weekends, starting at five P.M.

The wind was picking up, whitecaps appearing in the blue waters, and we were slipping our sweaters over our shoulders, stubbing out our cigarettes, looking down at our watches.

Then Powell Storm, Jr., was on his feet, heading our way, his hand suddenly around Mildred's arm. He wore a large, gold signet ring on one finger.

"Hey, miss? You got the order wrong."

First Mildred looked at his fingers on her arm, then jerked her arm away as though he had touched her with a hot poker.

"What's the matter?" He looked at her, really surprised. I don't think a girl'd ever pulled away from Powell Storm quite that way.

Mildred's face was a dark cloud.

"Don't. You. Touch. Me." The narrowed eyes, the jaw thrust forward.

Powell gave sort of a snort of a laugh—amazed, incredulous. He looked at those of us knitting there, as though we were a court of appeals, ran his long fingers through his thick black hair, held his hands out helplessly.

While he spoke, I tried to see the words written

across the face of the huge gold ring.

"All I was going to tell the lady was that my grandmother's not a gin drinker." He addressed himself to the knitters, while Mildred stood fuming beside my chair. "All I was going to tell the lady was that my grandmother'd like a plain lemonade."

Mildred again, this time between her teeth, "Tell the lady then, but keep your hands *off* the lady! I don't happen to like strangers mauling me!"

"*Mauling* you?" he said, while Mildred started away.

Back to the court of appeals. "Mauling her? Was I mauling her?"

"Do exactly what you did to her, to me, darling," Babs said, "and I'll try to give you a fair answer."

"Was I mauling her?" he was shouting. We were right in front of him. Mildred was on her way inside the clubhouse.

"I'm Powell Storm," he said.

We said our names and Babs said, "Sit down and have a ciggie poo with us."

He didn't take Babs up on her offer. He kept glancing over his shoulder, up at the clubhouse.

I kept trying to see what was written on his ring.

"Mildred doesn't mean anything," I said.

I was worrying for her, afraid she'd get a Storm mad at her and lose her job.

"Is that her name? Mildred what?"

"Cone," Molly said.

"C o h e n?"

"C o n e," Molly said. "Like in a pinecone?"

"Mauling her," he said, shaking his head, that snorty laugh again.

His face was still red. He sank his hands into the pockets of his shorts and rocked on the heels of his sneakers.

"Mildred's moody," I said. "That's all."

"Have one of my coffin nails," said Babs, leaning forward with her Chesterfields.

Powell shook his head, said he guessed he'd better get back to his family. "We've been treating Grandmother Dechepare to a little outing. She's been ill."

"She's real sweet-looking," Babs said. "She's a little doll!"

"How old *is* she?" Molly said.

Everyone was trying to keep Powell there.

"She's seventy-two," Powell said.

"Well, she's a marvel"—Babs.

Just as the accordion started playing, Mildred came back out of the clubhouse.

She was heading down toward the Storms' table, a single frosted glass on a tray, and she was walking mad. MAD might as well have been written in a little balloon over her head, the way words are over the heads of characters in comic strips. MAD. ANGRY. FURIOUS.

She wasn't looking right or left.

"Hey there! Millie!" Powell shouted.

"She doesn't like to have her name shortened," I tried to tell him, but he was too far from me to hear, running toward her on his long, tan, hairy legs.

The music was playing. The accordionist was singing.

Powell'd gone around in front of Mildred, trying to stop her in her tracks, his hands on the tray she was carrying. She tried to move ahead. He backed up a little. She tried to move sideways. He moved sideways with her. She tried to move back. He moved forward.

They were almost dancing.

". . . But there you were," the accordionist sang, "in love with me."

The song was none other than "I Had the Craziest Dream."

Suddenly both Powell and Mildred began laughing, their eyes shining at each other, stopped now, with a tray of lemonade the only thing between them.

Everyone was looking.

Even the Storms looked over at them. I still see their faces. The Storms were such good-looking people. You almost had the idea bad things shouldn't happen to people who looked like them, same as you felt worse when something bad happened to panda bears than you did when something bad happened to alligators.

I still see their beautiful faces, frozen in time, looking across at Powell and Mildred. When I see them that way, I think of it as the last time that family ever had a peaceful moment.

AUTHOR'S NOTE:
The title of the book, *I Stay Near You*, is written on the ring.

⊰ 3 ⊱

A Serial Writer

Fell

I often put real people in my books, but I always disguise them, giving them different names and sometimes different occupations. I never put anybody in a book in a way that discredits or embarrasses someone. This is not just because I have a kindly nature, but also because it could trigger a lawsuit and cost me more than the advance the publisher paid me.

Too bad, because the real story behind the Fell series is true, and even as I sketch it briefly for you, I have to omit and disguise some of the very bizarre circumstances.

After my graduation from the University of Missouri, I took an apartment with three sorority sisters. One of them was dating a young man who went to Yale; call him Winston Long. He had a big secret, which I found out by accident and promised never to tell.

Winston Long was enrolled at the university under a different name. He was paid by a very rich man to pose as his son, so that his son would inherit a large sum of money left by the grandfather. It was stipulated in the grandfather's will that the boy would come into his inheritance upon his graduation, as the third generation of Yale graduates.

An only child, this boy was intelligent enough to gain admission to Yale, but he was eccentric and phobic. He spent the four years on the family's ranch in Montana.

Winston earned the degree for him, then established a small advertising agency in San Francisco, with contacts and an endowment provided by his benefactor.

The four years of subterfuge were filled with narrow misses when Winston was almost found out and, after that, awkward encounters with old college acquaintances who'd wandered west, had chance encounters with him, and called out the name he no longer used.

I always knew someday, someway, I'd write about it.

My book *Gentlehands* had come about because I'd moved next door to a policeman's family. In that book I wrote about his son's first romance. But in the same way I knew someday I'd write about Winston, I knew that stories this policeman told me about local crime would be worked into a future novel.

As a former mystery/suspense writer, I'd always wanted to create a detective series. Why not invent a young man whose dad had been a detective? Let him get into perilous situations he gets out of using maneuvers learned from his detective dad.

I would begin the series with the same kind of offer Winston Long had been given. My boy would be paid for attending a school using another boy's identity.

First, he had to have the kind of name that could be worked into the books' titles. I decided to call him John Fell, because Fell was an easy name to play with.

The first book, *Fell*, would be followed by *Fell Back*, then *Fell Down*, on and on, until *Fell Over*, or *Fell Dead*. I also envisioned falling-down letters as part of the title:

F
  E
    L
     L

In the first book John Fell, a teenager and an amateur chef, meets the mysterious Woodrow Pingree, whose son, Thompson, is nicknamed Ping.

Mr. Pingree is a graduate of Gardner, a prep school where all Pingrees go. But Ping does not want to attend that school. He knows about The Tower, which all boys are made to climb up, and he is afraid of heights. Also, he suffers from asthma, and the small Pennsylvania town where the school is located has an abundance of ragweed.

Ping's Japanese-American stepmother, an artist, is determined to send Ping there. She is a cold, calculating woman who Ping believes murdered his real mother.

Ping wants to go far away from her, to L'Ecole la Coeur, in Switzerland.

"Change places with Ping," Mr. Pingree suggests to Fell. "You go to Gardner as him, and he'll go to school abroad, as you."

Fell is offered $10,000, and expenses, to do it.

There is a secret club called The Sevens at Gardner, and if Fell is asked to join it, he will get another $10,000. (No one can figure out how members are chosen. Maybe you can, from the brief glimpse of the school given here. If not, the answer is given in Chapter 18 of *Fell*.)

In these sample chapters, Fell begins his first few months at Gardner. His old girlfriend, Keats, thinks he's at the prep school in Switzerland. So, supposedly, does his new love, Delia Tremble, an au pair who has just embarked on a shipboard trip around the world. She is not the fun flirt she seems to be, but is part of a scheme Fell knows nothing about.

Unlike any other kind of book, a series requires a lot of planning before you sit down to write. You are going on a long journey with characters you must like writing about. Fell's detective dad is dead. There is just his mother and kid sister, Jazzy, and a doll Jazzy likes to dress up, named Georgette. I wish I'd made Jazzy older than five so she could become involved with Fell in future escapades. Once you've created your principal characters for a series, hindsight often nags at some of your choices.

Your people can be funny, loving, sly, or even malicious, but if there's one you feel you can't make interesting, you are stuck with him—for instance, Sidney Dibble, Fell's roommate. Sidney is one of my lucky names, which I use often, but I had no luck this time with this Sidney.

After I created him, I didn't like anything about him, including his nickname, Dib. I found him dull, and dreaded putting him into other books. There was nothing to do but kill him, which I did in *Fell Back*.

Here, then, is John Fell, disguised as the son of Woodrow Pingree.

from

⁕ Fell ⁕

The first thing I found out was that no one going to Gardner School ever called it that. They called it The Hill. The school sat on a hill in the middle of farm country. That was all I saw, once I got off the train at Trenton, New Jersey, and into the school bus. Ten of us new boys were bound for the little town of Cottersville, Pennsylvania.

There we were met by a dozen fellows in light-blue blazers and navy-blue pants. All the blazers had gold 7's over the blue-and-white Gardner insignias. The group formed a seven around us and sang the Gardner song.

> *Others will fill our places,*
> *Dressed in the old light blue.*
> *We'll recollect our races.*
> *We'll to the flag be true.*
> *And youth will still be in our faces*
> *When we cheer for a Gardner crew . . .*
> *And youth will still be in our faces*
> *When we cheer for a Gardner crew!*

A fellow behind me said, "Now we have to plant trees."

"We have to what?"

"We each have to plant a tree. It's the first thing you do when you get here, even before you get your room assigned. You get a little evergreen handed to you. You have to give it a name."

"What kind of a name?"

"Any name. A name. By the way, I'm Sidney Dibble. Dib."

"I'm Thompson Pingree. Tom."

He was the basketball player type, all legs and arms, skinny, so tall I had to look way up at him. He was blond like me. He had on a tan suit with a beige T-shirt and Reeboks.

169

I'd worn the only suit that had been mine in my other life: the dark-blue one. Pingree had driven me into New York City one August afternoon and taken me to Brooks Brothers. I had a whole trunkful of new stuff.

I asked Dib if he was sure about this tree thing. That was one detail Pingree'd left out. Dib said he was positive. His brother'd just graduated from Gardner. Dib said he was the world's foremost authority on Gardner—"Except when it comes to Sevens," he added.

The words weren't even out of his mouth a half second before a member of Sevens began barking orders at us. He was a tall skinhead, with vintage thrift-shop zoot-suit pants, and two earrings in his left ear. He had on a pair of black Converse sneakers.

"My name is Creery! Leave your luggage on the ground! It will be in your room when you get there! We will now walk back to Gardner Woods for the tree-planting ceremony! Think of a name for your tree on the way. Whatever you wish to call it. After you have planted your tree, you will line up to receive your room assignments in The Tower!"

"Who's the punk rocker?" I asked Dib. "I thought Sevens was this exclusive club?"

"He just told you. His name is Cyril Creery."

"And *he's* a Sevens?"

"There's no predicting who'll make Sevens. But he's easy. It's a guy named Lasher you don't want on your case. . . . unless *you* make Sevens. Then he can't touch you. Creery and Lasher hate each other. When Creery first got here, Lasher hated the sight of him. Creery had hair then. Purple hair. Lasher was out to get him. You know, Creery's the kind that named his tree Up Yours! Lasher would have made his life hell here, but Creery made Sevens."

"Don't the other members have a say in who makes Sevens?"

"I don't know how it works. No one does."

"Maybe you need three blackballs, like in a fraternity."

"Nobody knows," Dib said.

Besides the ten of us who'd gotten off the train in Trenton, there were ten other new boys already at The Hill. Now there were twenty of us walking to Gardner Woods.

There we found twenty holes in two rows, with twenty shovels beside them, and twenty mounds of dirt.

There was a line forming to receive the evergreens.

"You tell Creery the name of your tree, then stick it in the ground and throw the dirt over it," Dib said. "I'm going to name mine after my dog, Thor."

"Are all those trees in the background from classes ahead of us?"

"You've got it. What are you naming yours?"

"I'm not sure yet."

"You better have a name ready when we get up there."

I thought of naming mine Delia. But that wouldn't have been the way we'd agreed to be. Nothing permanent. A tree was pretty permanent. I thought of all the names people called their houses down on Dune Road in Seaville. I thought of Keats's house, Adieu. I thought of Keats's saying on Labor Day, "Daddy says you can come here as long as you've come to say good-bye." I told her she could tell Daddy to shove it! Keats said, "Oh, my, my, my. Aren't we arrogant now that we're going abroad to school. Do you kiss arrogantly now, too?" I didn't kiss her good-bye arrogantly, but I did try to get something simulating emotion into it. Nothing. Delia'd have laughed. She'd have said, "What did you think, Fell, that you could forget me?"

I said to Dib, "I may name mine Adieu."

"Oh, oui?" He laughed.

"No, not Adieu," I said. "Good-bye."

"Your tree's going to be called Good-bye?"

"It's as good as Thor, isn't it?"

"Sure. Call it anything. You know this guy Lasher I told you about? My brother says he puts on this big act. He wants to be a playwright. He writes these plays with characters in them named Death and Destruction, like he thinks he's profound, but it's all a lot of bullticky crap! I mean, he's a vegetarian, and he works out, and he's this big hypochondriac, but he's always playing with nooses and pretending he's being called to the grave. Well, he named his tree Suicide."

"I'm going to call mine Good-bye."

Good-bye to John Fell and his life, but not good-bye to Delia Tremble. We were going to write. "Promise," she'd said, "and if you don't like to write letters, or if you think you probably won't write me once you get there, tell me right now. I don't want false expectations."

I said I'd write. I promised.

Keats'd said, "Are we going to write ever?"

"I don't know," I'd said.

"Do you know you've changed since June? I'm going to think you've met someone else."

I couldn't tell her about it.

I was afraid I'd jinx it if I told anyone about Delia. "Jinx *what*?" my mother'd said. "She's going away for a year and all July and August you never knew when you were going to see her."

"Men! Plant your trees!" Creery shouted after we'd all been given an evergreen.

Men? The last time I'd ever been in on a tree planting was back in grade school in Brooklyn one Arbor Day. We'd all sung "This Land Is Your Land!" and walked around this little cherry tree holding hands.

Something about being one of ten boys in line with silver shovels and our holes already dug for us, with ten of the same behind us, reminded me of third grade.

But later, what happened in The Tower, didn't.

He said Sevens were always called by their last names, so I would call him Lasher. Everyone else on The Hill, except for faculty, was called by their first name. Good, I thought! No Pingree.

He said I'd been assigned to him. I was in his group. If I ever needed anything, I'd ask him if I could have it.

He had very thick glasses, like Ping's. He had thick, coal-black hair like Delia's, but his was cut very short. He had one of those almost beards— stubble, really—and a stubble mustache. A smile that tipped to one side.

How much older than me? A year maybe. Maybe

my age. Seventeen. But I was sixteen at Gardner School. I wasn't a Gemini anymore, either. I was a horny Scorpio. Don't ask me how Ping could be a Scorpio with all the sex appeal of a can opener, but he was. So was I, now.

Lasher said, "What'd you name your tree?"

"Good-bye."

"Good-bye's its name or are you a smartass?"

"That's its name."

We were way up in The Tower. We had to go up one at a time, alphabetically. One hundred and twenty steps. The stairs were stone ones on the outside. Even if you didn't have a fear of heights it wasn't a climb that set your heart to singing.

In the top of The Tower was this one stone-walled room, lit by a single candle on the table. Lasher sat at the table. There was nowhere for me to sit. I stood. Lasher had on a white tank top under his blazer.

"Thompson, I want to tell you something. Don't screw up! You've been assigned to me. I hate having scumbags who come here and can't take it or can't make it! I happen to hate legacies, too—types like Creery, whose father *and* grandfather went here, and miraculously all got to be Sevens! I happen to love this place . . . *and* Sevens! It's a privilege to be here, not a right! Act like you wanted to come here more than you wanted to get laid the first time, and we'll get along."

"I'll do that."

"You have gotten yourself laid by now, haven't you?"

"Yes, I have."

"Good. I won't have to cart you out to Willing Wanda's to get laid. I don't like virgins under my charge. Virgins are vulnerable. I don't like vulnerable scumbags under my charge! *Latet anguis in herba*, Thompson! Do you know your Latin?"

"I don't know what that means."

"It's from Virgil. It means the snake hides in the grass. It's my motto."

"Okay," I said.

I could see that the gold buttons on his blazer had little 7's on them.

Then he said, "Seven Seas: the Arctic and the Antarctic. North and South Pacific. North and South Atlantic. The Indian Ocean."

I didn't know what that meant. I stood there.

"If a Sevens meets you he might ask you to name seven things that go together. If you can't think of seven things that go together, he might ask you to clean all the toilets in Hull House, where you'll be living. He might ask you to do anything, if you can't come up with seven things, and you'll have to do it!"

"All right," I said. "I'll find seven things for an answer."

"Find a lot of seven things. You can't repeat."

"All right."

"Your roommate is sixteen. He's from New Hope, Pennsylvania. He's a legacy, too."

"Okay," I said.

Lasher took off his thick glasses while he continued and talked with his eyes shut, as though he was bored out of his gourd but he had to get through this.

"Your roommate is a virgin. Your roommate called me sir all through his interview. Your roommate named his tree after his puppy dog. He lets people call him Dib, a boy's nickname. He's obviously still on Pablum, so grow him up, Thompson, because your roommate's a vulnerable scumbag who doesn't realize *latet anguis*—finish it, Thompson!" He opened his eyes and looked up at me.

"In the grass . . . *in herba*."

So I was rooming with Sidney Dibble.

Lasher gave me this smile that was as beautiful as he was, without those thick glasses.

"Welcome to The Hill!" Lasher said.

✼

John Fell
L'Ecole la Coeur
C H—1092 Rolle
Lake Geneva
Switzerland
Dear F
     E
       L

     L [I liked the way she wrote my name falling down], *I'll never forget our last dinner at The Frog Pond, remember? You were so sunburned you couldn't lean back in your chair. I liked it because you had to lean toward me.*

    I know we said we wouldn't write about ordinary happenings—my idea, because I want our memories to be of what we shared together, but I want to know certain things about you . . . if you like where you are . . . if you are glad you made the choice to go to Switzerland. . . . You must tell me those things. . . . Tell me a thought you haven't told anyone. I won't tell you about life on this ship, except to say one port is like the next, and I think of you. I remember once you combed your hair after we were down on the beach. You put the comb in your back pocket, looked over at me and said, "Do I look all right?" I love it that you gave me that unguarded moment. "Do I look all right?" you asked me. . . . I don't write long letters, F

$$E$$

$$L$$

$$L,$$

but I think long thoughts. Love, Delia.

The envelope Ping had sent it in was addressed to W. Thompson Pingree, Gardner School, Cottersville, Pennsylvania, U.S.A.

There were two letters from my mother inside. Even she had to write to me in Switzerland, where Ping would forward her mail. Pingree had insisted.

There was also a note from Ping.

Your French is improving,
but you are avoiding all courses in computer science.
How am I doing?
Have I been up in The Tower yet?

I was rereading my mail in Hull House on a Sunday morning in October, anxious to get a letter off to Delia before "my father" arrived. It was Pingree's first visit. He was going to chapel with me.

"Just think," Dib said behind me, "right now, in that luxurious clubhouse in the bottom of The Tower, there's the aroma of rib roast cooking for the Sevens to enjoy after chapel! They'll have rib roast and mashed potatoes. We'll be lucky to have chicken again. They've got it made, haven't they?"

"One thing I'm sick of," I said, "is everyone's obsession with the Sevens! God, who are they that everyone runs around in awe of them?"

"Wouldn't you like to be one?"

"Only because of all their privileges."

"And their meals."

"That's part of their privileges."

"They're like another race," Dib said. "The Master Race."

Dib was munching on some Black Crows. He was always eating. Eating stuff like Hostess Ding Dongs, M&M's, Fruit Bars, and Sno-Caps. Dib was like most kids who'd rather eat Whoppers at Burger King than duckling à l'orange at the best French restaurant. He thought frozen Lean Cuisine was gourmet food, and a box of Sara Lee double chocolate layer cake was a better dessert than fresh-made key lime pie. It wasn't just the food Sevens were privileged to have, that we weren't, that got to Dib. It was the whole aura of Sevens, and it got to everyone. Everyone at Gardner envied them, watched them, gossiped about them, and wished they were part of them.

The night before, Lasher had taken Dib out to Willing Wanda's for Dib's sexual initiation.

When he came back, Dib said, "Did you ever

hear an old song called 'Is That All There Is?'"

"Yes. Some woman named Peggy Lee made a record of it. My mom loved it."

"In it, this kid sees a fire and says is that all there is to a fire?"

"Right."

"That's how I felt about what went on at Willing Wanda's."

"You'll feel more when you're in love."

"I hope so. I'd rather eat a box of Mallomars or dig into a plate of Chicken McNuggets."

"Chicken McNuggets," I said, and I put two fingers down my throat and retched.

Dib was working on his paper for the New Boys Competition. There were always rumors about how one got tapped for Sevens, and one of them was that the N.B.C. had something to do with it. All new students were required to write a paper by the last day of October. The theme that year was "They All Chose America." You could choose any group that'd immigrated. Dib was doing the Irish. I got the bright idea to do Japanese Americans, and to call mine "Arizona Darkness."

I had only the title and some books from the library about President Roosevelt's executive order 9066, which sent 150,000 Japanese Americans to concentration camps back in World War Two. They were given less than forty-eight hours to gather their possessions together for evacuation. Although there were three times as many Americans of Italian descent living on the West Coast, they weren't affected. Neither were German Americans. Only Japanese.

I wanted to answer Delia's letter before I worked on that.

Dib said, "Name some famous Irish Americans."

"How about the Kennedys?"

"I've got them."

"I want to write a letter before my father gets here," I said, "so don't talk to me, okay?"

"Dear Delia," Dib said, "how are things in Switzerland?"

He thought that's where she was, and that was why I got mail from Switzerland. I let him think it.

Dear Delia [I wrote],

Last week in Classics we read Aeschylus's account of Clytemnestra's welcoming Agamemnon home from the Trojan War. She asked him to walk the last few yards on a purple carpet of great value. He didn't want to do it. He said it was too valuable to walk on. But she insisted. Then he went inside the palace and she murdered him in his bath. . . . I thought of when a girl I loved gave me a purple bow tie, then stood me up for the Senior Prom. . . .

I got an A+ for the paper I wrote about it.

I thought, I'm glad she's in my past. I'm glad there's Delia.

A secret thought. Oscar Wilde once wrote he who expects nothing will never be disappointed. I don't expect anything from you, Delia. Will you ever disappoint me?

I'm not sorry about choosing to come to L'Ecole la Coeur. So far, so good. That night at The Frog Pond? My back wasn't that sunburned. I wanted to lean into you.

Love, F

E

L

L

I addressed the letter c/o The Worldwide Tours Group, Goodship Cruise, San Francisco, California, for forwarding. Then I put that letter into an envelope addressed to John Fell at L'Ecole la Coeur. Ping would mail it for me.

Just as I was finishing, the buzzer rang three short, one long, my signal.

"Your dad's here," said Dib.

I hadn't seen or talked to Pingree since early September. I never called him, though I'd memorized his phone number in case of emergency. He didn't even want me to write it in my address book. That was just one of his rules, along with others like no photographs of myself at Gardner ever. He said to take sick the day they scheduled class pictures for the yearbook. Avoid all cameras!

I wore the new tan gabardine suit he'd bought me. He had on a dark, vested, pin-striped one.

"What a day!" he said. It was warm and the sun was out. "I'm glad to see you, my boy! I'm glad you're doing so well!"

I walked along beside him, down the path toward chapel.

"I haven't gone below A since I've been here, so it must agree with me. I'm not repeating that much, either. It's harder here than it was in public school."

"Your monthly report was excellent, Fell! That paper you did for Classics, what did you call it? The one you got an A+ on?"

" 'The Purple Carpet.' Did they mention that?"

"Dr. Skinner reported that you have a flair for composition. I even showed it to Fern, because of the carpet business. That would be like Ping, you know. He was always intrigued by magic carpets. *The Arabian Nights*. It sounded like Ping."

"It didn't have anything to do with *The Arabian Nights*," I said.

"It doesn't matter. Fern thought it did. She said, 'You see, I was right. He got past all that Tower business.' " Pingree chuckled. He clapped his arm around my shoulder, an inch of ash dropping off his cigarette. "It's working out. You're doing fine!"

"And Ping?"

"He loves it over there! When I spoke to him last night on the telephone, I said, 'Complain a little more. You don't sound like yourself.'"

In chapel, the Gardner choir sang:

> And youth will still be in our faces
> When we cheer for a Gardner crew.
> Yes, youth will still be in our faces
> We'll remain to Gardner true!

Pingree wiped tears from his eyes.

After, Pingree said, "I can't stay for Sunday dinner. I don't want to get involved up here, anyway. But good Lord, it takes me back to walk around this place!"

"How are things in Seaville?"

"The same. Is your mother happy in Brooklyn?"

"They still can't find a decent apartment. But she says it's so good to be a subway ride from Macy's again she doesn't care."

We both chuckled, and then he stopped as he saw The Tower.

"Ah! The Tower!"

"Do you want to walk over there?" I asked him. "My roommate says they're cooking rib roast down in the Sevens's clubhouse for Sunday dinner."

"Yes, their Sunday dinners are always the envy of everyone. Steak Wednesday nights, so they say. The inside of that clubhouse is supposed to be very elegant! No, I'll just admire it from a distance, as I always did."

We started walking along again.

"What did you name your tree?" I asked him.

"My tree. I almost forgot about planting that tree."

"That was one thing you didn't warn me about."

"I completely forgot. You plant it, you forget it. I named mine Sara. That was my first wife's name."

"You knew her way back then?"

"Oh yes. Way back then." He lit another cigarette. "She went to Miss Tyler's in Princeton. You would have liked her. She was always questioning what it all meant. What we were put on this earth for, all that sort of thing. She was a philosophy major. She was my first melancholy baby. Do you know that song?"

"No."

"You don't know 'Melancholy Baby'?"

"No, I don't."

"I can't believe they don't still sing it."

"Maybe they do. I don't know it. I guess Delia's a melancholy baby, too. She doesn't sound like she loves the trip she's on."

"Ah, yes. Delia."

"We write," I said.

"Well, good."

"She's going around the world. Did I tell you that?"

"Yes, you did. Do you really love this Delia, Fell?"

"I don't know."

"That's good, that you don't know."

"Why is it good?"

"Love is such an interference. When it happens to you, you let your guard down. You should never let your guard down."

"I guess you're right," I said. I don't know what he was thinking of, but I was thinking of Keats, and how she'd treated me once she could take me for granted. . . . I still hadn't written to Keats.

"You know, Fell—I should call you Thompson around here, or Tom—I've grown very fond of you."

"Thanks," I said. "I like you, too."

"I'm going to travel next month, and I got worried over the idea what if something happens to me? Where would that leave you? So I've already transferred the first ten thousand to a savings account for you. Here's your book."

"Aren't you afraid I'll skip out on you now that I have the money?" I laughed.

"No. I trust you. I know you won't touch it until your year is over. Your allowance is sufficient, isn't it?"

"Yes, and I have some extra from selling the Dodge."

I took a look at the bankbook. It was from the Union Trust Company in Brooklyn Heights. John T. Fell.

Pingree said, "I was going to put the money in trust for you, in your mother's name."

"I'm glad you didn't. MasterCard would get their hands on it, or Visa, or some collection agency. My mother owes all over the place."

"I realize that. And you're a big boy. We have to trust each other, don't we, Fell?"

"Yes, we do," I agreed. "I'm working hard on the French, too. By Christmas I'll *sound* like I've been going to L'Ecole la Coeur."

"I'm not worried about you," he said. He let the cigarette drop from his mouth, stepped on it, and said, "Walk me down to my car. I love this place, you know. I was happiest right here."

November. I was out in front of Hull House one afternoon reading a letter from Keats. Even if it hadn't been written to me, and wasn't signed, I would have known it was Keats's, right away.

Dear Fell,

Here's a poem I translated for Spanish, written by Pedro Calderon de La Barca (1600–1681).

> *And what is life but frenzy?*
> *And what is it but fancy?*
> *A shadow, mere fiction,*
> *for its greatest good is small,*
> *and life itself a dream,*
> *and dreams are only dreams.*

Doesn't that make you really depressed, Fell? So why am I writing you? It won't help my mood to remember that you caught me out in everything, from going to the prom with Quint to his coming to Four Winds that weekend . . . and you never forgave me. I don't blame you. . . . But I was in Seaville last weekend to see Seaville High play Northport (I'll always go back for that game). They lost, which was depressing, too. They only won two games the whole season!

Oh, Fell, I'm never going to be supportive of anyone. I'm always going to need it and never be able to give it, which makes me practically worthless!

One thing I did do when I was home, went to the Stiles Gallery. Maybe just because I'd heard you dated their summer au pair and hoped she'd show up there, so I could get a look at her.

Fell, I'm not over you yet, although I gave you every indication I was. I dream of your smell. The scent awakens me like a ghost tickling my nose with a thread from its sheet.

Also, Mrs. Pingree's work was on display. Early Works, they were called. Smiles We Left Behind Us *was there, just as peculiar as you'd described it, but even more weird was the painting of seaweed. Just this orange seaweed under green water. Well, that is not the shock. She called it* Sara. *It is really strange, Mummy says, because when the first Mrs. Pingree died (her name was Sara!), there were rumors Fern Pingree pushed her overboard. She couldn't swim. She drowned. . . . Seaweed . . . Sara . . . How about that for weird? It's 10X weirder than anything going on in my life, which is at a depressing standstill. Is yours?*

Do you speak French fluently now? I saw L'Ecole la Coeur advertised in the back of Town and Country. *Très chic!*

> *Je t'adore! Toujours,*
> *Keats.*

Then from behind me someone shouted, "SEVENS!"

I whirled around. It was Lasher glaring down at me through those thick glasses.

I was supposed to answer with seven things that went together. "Grammar," I said, trying to remember all the seven sciences, "Logic, Arithmetic, Music, Geometry, Astronomy, and . . . and . . ."

"*And?*" Lasher said. "Are you naming the seven medieval sciences?"

"Yes."

"Well, what have you left out?"

"I don't know."

"You left out Rhetoric, Thompson!"

Lasher had on an old tweed topcoat, with the collar up. He had his stubble beard with his stubble mustache. I wished my father'd lived to see stubble get to be an in thing. My father used to come home from all-night jobs unshaved, complaining that he looked like some bum.

"Okay," I said. "The seven names of God. El, Elohim—"

Lasher cut me off. "No second chances, Thompson!"

He came around to face me, his hands sunk in his pockets. The wind blew back his thick black hair. I could never see his eyes. The leaves were off the trees above us. It was a blustery late-fall afternoon.

I was cold in just a yellow turtleneck sweater and tan cords.

"I want you to go to The Tower after your dinner tonight," said Lasher, "and place a lighted candle on every step. You'll find the candles and their ceramic holders in a carton outside the Sevens clubhouse. Do you understand, Thompson?"

"What about study hall?"

"Just tell the proctor you're on a Sevens assignment. Get your ass there by seven-thirty. Seventhirty, sharp, scumbag!"

"All right."

"You go all the way to the top. Then press the clubhouse bell so we can all come out and admire your handiwork before you blow them all out on your way back down."

"All right."

"Stupid!" Lasher growled as he walked away. "You left out Rhetoric!"

It was a Wednesday. We always had a test at the start of French on Thursday mornings. I usually studied hard on Wednesday nights. I wouldn't that Wednesday night. Not after one hundred and twenty steps.

"He's really a sadist," Dib said. "I have a theory about why he is."

"Why is he?"

Dib was eating a Baby Ruth, getting ready for dinner. Our room in Hull House looked as if burglars had just left it. Dib never closed a door he opened, or picked up anything he took off. We never had room inspections. No one ever got on our backs about whether or not the beds were made. The only tyranny at Gardner was Sevens.

"He's mean because God gave him that one flaw," Dib said. "His eyesight. That's the real snake in the grass."

"He ought to get contact lenses. His eyes are real pretty."

"He can't wear them. He gets allergic to anything in his eyes. Creery says if Lasher didn't have to wear those glasses you could shave him, put a dress on him, and ask him to go out on a date."

"Except he wouldn't go out with Creery," I said. "Creery's too much of a stonehead."

"Creery says he's mean because both his parents are shrinks, and shrinks' kids are always messes. Sevens is his real family—that's why he makes so much of it. He's been in Sevens since he was fourteen."

"Maybe he's mean because his family shipped him out when he was so young."

"Or maybe," said Dib, "his family shipped him out when he was so young because he was mean."

The dinner bell rang and we went downstairs and walked across the commons together.

"I'd be a little scared to go up in The Tower by myself after dark," Dib said.

"I'm not looking forward to it."

"You should have packed your gun."

"I never carry it or load it."

"Yeah. Guns scare the hell out of me, too."

"I know a girl who got turned on by the sight of that gun."

"Delia?"

"Yeah, Delia."

"Why don't you have a picture of her?"

"We never took any."

"Ask her for one. I'd like to see this Trembling Delia."

"I've asked her and asked her."

In my last letter to her, I underlined my request in red. When she answered it, she wrote:

Oh, don't tell me you've forgotten how I look, F

E

L

L.

That was all. I shook the envelope to be sure she hadn't put a photograph inside. She hadn't.

I sometimes thought if I hadn't been assigned to Dib for a roommate, I'd walk everywhere alone at

Gardner. I wasn't good at making friends with kids whose smiles and clothes and walks shouted money, prep school, connections, tennis!

Dib and I were two of a kind that way. He didn't make friends easily, either. His father wasn't a captain of industry. His father was the great-grandson of one. He drank a lot and raised orchids and a brand of wrinkle-faced dogs called Chinese sharpeis. Dib's brother had gone from Gardner to a seminary, to become a priest.

Dib said his mother was strange, too. She went to séances and hunted ducks they raised on their farm for her to hunt.

He'd asked me once if my family was strange. He'd said your father didn't look it, in chapel. What you know about someone from looking at him is zilch, I'd said, but I'd played down my family. I'd just said they were both physicists. I'd said my mother painted.

On the way to dinner that night he asked me how come a physicist had a gun like that?

My one slip. The gun. I'd told Dib my father'd given it to me.

"He's a collector," I said.

"I hope you're not from Mafia," Dib said. "That gun looked like something the Godfather'd pack. Are you sure your real name isn't Pingratti?"

I laughed hard and felt my knees go weak. "No. My real name's not Pingratti," I said.

After dinner I told the proctor I had a Sevens assignment.

"In that case . . ." He shrugged. You could get away with anything at Gardner if Sevens said so.

I walked over to The Tower. The campus lights were on.

I could smell steak. We'd had Spanish rice and beets for dinner.

I could see inside the Sevens clubhouse, where the curtains fell apart in one window near the bottom of the steps.

I looked in.

It was like some kind of movie set in there. MGM filming King Arthur's Court, only the knights were all in light-blue blazers and black top hats. It looked like a convention of chimney sweeps.

There were enough silver candelabras set out on the long dinner table to make Liberace look chintzy. There were four waiters running around in white jackets. I could see floor-to-ceiling bookcases all around the room, and a roaring fire inside a walk-in stone fireplace.

I could see Creery in there with a hand-painted palm tree tie around the neck of one of those formal shirts usually worn under tuxedo jackets. He looked like his old goofy self, the top hat covering his shaved head, two razor-blade earrings dangling from his left earlobe.

I got to work.

I pulled over the carton near the stairs, and began my ascent. I had to drag the carton up with me. There were oven matches inside, and the ceramic holders were tall enough to keep the candles from blowing out in the wind.

I thought about Mom and Jazzy, wishing I could get to Brooklyn for Thanksgiving. I used to always make the stuffing, a corn-bread one with sausage and mushrooms. I longed to cook again. Mom had a job as a hostess in a restaurant down near the World Trade Center in New York City. She was looking for something in catering or fancy food. She'd written that she made just enough money to last the month, unless she bought something. She'd write *Ha! Ha!* after one of her jokes. She'd put it in parentheses. Sometimes she'd write *(Sob!)* . . . *I miss you (Sob!)*. She said Jazzy was working on costumes for Georgette, since soon Georgette was going to discover her real parents were Rumanian royalty. *(She pronounces it "Woomanian." She thinks they dress in furs and crowns.)*

Sometimes in his sleep, Dib would whimper and cry, "Mommy? Are you there?" He'd get me thinking. Are you there, Mommy? Jazzy? Georgette?

I thought of Delia, too. Delia with the slow smile and long kisses, dancing on the wet grass to "Don't Go Changing."

I thought of Keats going to the Stiles Gallery, and I thought of a lot of orange seaweed in green water, called *Sara*.

When I was at the top of The Tower, I looked down at all the candles, and I remembered once when the Stileses went out, we'd let the candles burn down in their living room, Delia and I, while we held each other on the long, beige sofa.

It was the first time I'd told her I loved her.

"Don't make me say I love you, Fell."

"Who said you had to say it?"

"I thought you'd expect it because you said it."

"I did, but I'm not going to stay awake nights if you don't say it." I stayed awake a lot of nights because she didn't say it. I knew I would when I said I wasn't going to stay awake nights if she didn't say it.

Just as I was about to go inside the room at the top of The Tower to ring the clubhouse bell, I heard Lasher's voice behind me. I jumped. He held me with his hand around my neck.

"Thompson, look down there at the ground and

tell me if it makes you want to jump."

"No, I don't want to jump." My heart was racing. How'd he get up there?

"I named my tree Suicide, Thompson."

"I heard you did. If you want to jump, let go of me first." He held me near the edge of the wall, and I thought, He's crazy. I'm up here by myself with this maniac.

Then Creery's voice came like a sweet release. "Knock it *off*, Lasher!"

Lasher let go of me.

Creery had a lantern flashlight. He was shutting a gate in the little stone-walled room behind us. It was the first time I knew anything about an inside elevator in The Tower.

Creery pushed the clubhouse bell.

It rang out in the windy night. There was a moon overhead, with clouds passing through its face— now you see it, now you don't. Below us, there were shouts as the Sevens poured out of their clubhouse.

Creery put the lantern on the table. He picked up a bullhorn and walked out to where we were.

"SEVENS!" Creery shouted.

Then the Sevens shouted up in thinner voices: "Wisdom! Understanding! Counsel! Power! Knowledge! Righteousness! Godly fear!"

Creery led the singing.

> *The time will come as the years go by,*
> *When my heart will thrill*
> *At the thought of The Hill . . .*

While they sang the song, I remembered something my father'd once said, that anything that is too stupid to be spoken is sung. But it was then that Lasher stopped singing and started talking while they sang, grabbing my shoulders with his hands; behind him, Creery's razor-blade earrings bobbed as he sang and shook his head up and down.

Lasher was calling me Pingree.

"You made Sevens, Pingree!"

Creery said, "Congratulations, Pingree!"

> *And the Sevens who came*
> *With their bold cry,*
> *WELCOME TO SEVENS, I*

Lasher and Creery had turned me around so I stood looking down at the candles in the wind, with the moon shifting above us, the sounds of their singing, the lights of Gardner scattered over The Hill.

> *Remember the cry.*
> *WELCOME TO SEVENS!*

Below, with their top hats flying into the night,

they shouted seven times: "PINGREE! PINGREE! PINGREE! PINGREE! PINGREE! PINGREE! PINGREE!"

Then Creery said, "We'll take the elevator down to our clubhouse, Pingree."

"Sevens don't walk when they don't have to," Lasher said. Then he smiled at me. "Surprised you, didn't we, Pingree?"

⌇ 4 ⌇

Must You Be a Cake to Write a Cookbook?

Little Little

Before I wrote books for kids, I wrote mystery and suspense, often through the eyes of the criminal. It never occurred to me that I wasn't qualified to use the felon viewpoint since I had no experience as a thief, a kidnapper, or a murderer. That was my job: to write in whatever voice was best for the story. Young, old, male, female, I was never self-conscious in any guise.

When I began writing YA literature, I told my stories with the same bravado. Then I had a conversation with the distinguished black author Walter Dean Myers, whom I met at a conference of children's writers and editors. I'd just finished *Love Is a Missing Person*, about a romance between a black and a white teenager. Walter told me he'd read it, and I asked him what he thought about the black characters I'd created.

"Well," he said, in a noncommittal tone, with a shrug, "they were different."

I wasn't sure then what he meant, but a while later, older and wiser, I understood.

A black girl in the book said things like this: "Oh, honey, honey, I'd like to die imagining you without your allowance, child. . . . Lord take pity on you, without your 'lowance, you gonna be reduced to poverty level."

A bit of a stereotype.

The boy, however, was tipped so far back the other way, I was reminded of the black man the white woman in the movie *Guess Who's Coming to Dinner* brought home to meet her parents, Katharine Hepburn and Spencer Tracy. Sidney Poitier played this handsome, brilliant brain surgeon.

My boy, Roger Coe III, was a blue-eyed, six-foot black, who was a straight-A student with ambitions to be an engineer. He was the halfback star of the football team, a track, baseball, and tennis star, as well as a pole vaulter.

The white girl adds, "I think he could be a movie star."

In the movie, Sidney Poitier didn't have to be a brain surgeon to pass family inspection. And in *Love Is a Missing Person* Roger Coe didn't need a III after his name, plus all the rest, to be a suitable swain for a white girl.

The black girl commenting on her white friend's allowance didn't need to talk in dialect, either.

You would think I would have been too embarrassed to ever again write about anyone but a female, white, Anglo-Saxon Protestant.

But writers learn by making mistakes, and grow by broadening hackneyed viewpoints.

You don't have to be a cake to write a cookbook, but you do have to know a bit about the ingredients in your recipes.

We are informed by our times, too. Now we say Native American, instead of Indian; Asian instead of Oriental; and sometimes we don't even say black anymore, but African American.

A writer today can become so self-conscious about political correctness that the old children's game of Cowboys and Indians becomes Cowpeople and Native Americans.

Still, as the writer becomes better informed, he must not become intimidated to the point of never including in his books characters who are unlike him in color, religion, ethnic background, or sexual orientation.

Teachers tell kids, "Write about what you know!"—good advice—but it shouldn't stop you if there's something that really interests you that you don't know that much about.

The Gulf War interested me. It is the only war we were involved in that happened in the lifetime of today's kids. Although it was a short war, some of them can still remember the yellow ribbons and American flags people wore . . . and some can remember the computer-game look of it on television. More know one or another family member who fought in that war, and still today feel the far-reaching effects of whatever went on in the sands of Saudi Arabia.

I wasn't a soldier in the Gulf, but I am a fairly accomplished researcher, and my research produced *Linger*. It is the story of three young men who went to the war, and the two who survived.

The hardest book I ever wrote was one called *Little Little*, about a pair of teenage dwarfs.

I am not handicapped, and I am five foot five.

What made the book difficult for me was that I wanted my three-going-on-four-foot characters to be sympathetic but not sentimentalized. I didn't want readers to pity them, and I didn't want readers to think they had nothing in common with them. All of us have experienced prejudice, and those of us who have had more than our share of it develop a sense of humor, a survivor's humor. I wanted my dwarfs to reflect that, but not to come off as bitter or beaten down.

I had to have just the right voices for my two lead characters, and they had to have just the right names.

I stopped and started the book many times before I felt secure enough to continue.

Sydney Cinnamon was the name I finally came up with for my humpbacked, orphaned seventeen-year-old. He works for a pest control company, wearing a cockroach costume, and appears in TV commercials and at shopping centers and the openings of bowling alleys and cut-rate liquor stores. He is something of a star, with his own theme song, "La Cucaracha," and his own groupies.

He is everything the parents of my second dwarf detest. He is not perfectly formed (not p.f.) and he lets himself be exploited, put on display, and laughed at. He is the opposite of the girl I call Belle La Belle, nicknamed Little Little. She *is* p.f., almost eighteen, a beautiful heiress whose parents hope to find her a suitable match. Educated, witty, at the beginning of the book she is about to have a birthday party, with dwarfs from all over invited.

In the first chapter we discover that Sydney will be there too. In the second we meet Little Little, and in the third, Sydney has his first glimpse of her.

In this book I use alternating chapters so the reader has both the male's viewpoint and the female's.

Later books are almost all from the male's point of view, and when I speak to kids, they want to know why this is.

Teachers have told me that boys prefer to read only stories that boys tell. Girls like both. So if I use a male voice, then everyone's happy.

from

⋇ Little Little ⋇

Sydney Cinnamon

"Sydney," Mr. Palmer said, "you are on your way to becoming the most famous dwarf in this country, no small thanks to me. And now I have a favor to ask you."

Those words, spoken on an ordinary August day, in the offices of Palmer Pest Control, were the beginning of my new life.

So far, age seventeen, I had had two other beginnings. One was my birth and abandonment to The Twin Oaks Orphans' Home in Wilton, New York.

One was my first appearance as The Roach, mascot for the Wilton Bombers, at halftime during the first game of the year. I was fifteen, and though I didn't know it at the time, it was to be the last year I'd attend Wilton High School.

"Sydney Cinnamon," Mr. Palmer said that morning in his office, "with everything against you, you made yourself into something. You created a self for yourself. You are The Roach, an entity of your own invention, and I admire you for it. I have something along the same order in mind for myself."

"What are you planning to become?" I asked him.

"I'm not planning to become anything. I'm planning on Palmer Pest Control becoming something. I want to go national, Sydney! I want to be big!" Mr. Palmer looked like an enormous bird, like the kind of huge, skinny, long-beaked bird that swooped down from the sky, poked around in the dirt, and carried away the very creatures Mr. Palmer exterminated for a living.

"Sydney," he said, rubbing his palms together ecstatically, "I'm negotiating with a Japanese named Hiroyuki for a merger with Twinkle Traps, over in La Belle, New York. Together, Twinkle and Palmer could control the market. I need your help, Sydney."

He knew he could ask me to do anything. Because of him, I had changed from an orphaned dwarf who picked up odd jobs jumping out of birthday cakes, or working summers at resorts like Leprechaun Village, to a TV personality who earned enough money to finally order clothes made that fit, and furniture my own size.

The commercials I made for P.P.C., as The Roach, were famous in upstate New York. If Mr. Palmer had exaggerated slightly in saying I was on my way to becoming the most famous dwarf in the country, it still did not take away from the fact I had my own little fame wherever I went.

And fame is fame. The big fish in the little pond doesn't bother its head about larger bodies of water. Thanks to Albert Palmer, I'd gone from entertaining as The Roach at halftime in high school football fields to making commercials and appearing at shopping centers, and starring at openings of everything from bowling alleys to cut-rate liquor stores.

I even had my own theme song, which was "La Cucaracha," and my own groupies, kids who congregated wherever I appeared, and waved pieces of paper at me that they wanted me to autograph.

"I'll do anything you say," I told Mr. Palmer, and he rubbed his bald head and grinned at me, then came around and sat on the front of his desk, facing me.

"The last week in September," he said, "the Wilton Bombers are playing the La Belle Boots, at La Belle. Sydney, I'd like you to make an appearance at halftime. It's a way to tell our home team you haven't forgotten your beginnings, and we're still in there rooting for them. And it's a way to show you off in La Belle."

"That's easy," I said.

"And the second part isn't going to be hard, either. There's a surprise in it for you, Sydney, one I think you'll like. She's your size, Sydney."

"Who?"

"They call her Little Little La Belle. She's one of the little people, like you, and she's the daughter of Larry La Belle. Of course, his family is very prominent in that town, town's named for them. She's having her eighteenth birthday party that weekend, and Mr. Hiroyuki would like you to make a little surprise guest appearance at the party. His boy's a friend of the family, and that'd be his gift to this little girl."

"It's all right with me," I said.

"You'll be a surprise for the little lady, and it'll help me get Hiroyuki in a good mood when we talk merger."

I said I would and then I began wangling for the very best accommodations while I was in La Belle.

I'd learned to do that from a fellow named Knox Lionel. We'd roomed together in the employees' dormitory at Leprechaun Village, the summer we both worked there. Knox was seventeen that summer and I was fourteen. He was a combination philosopher and con man, who loved to watch the TV preachers and imitate them. He entertained us in the dorm posing as a preacher called Opportunity Knox, a mixture of all the television preachers he'd studied. He could beam like Robert Schuller and shake a pointed finger like Billy Graham. He stood on a box to deliver sermons on sin that had us holding our sides laughing.

But he wasn't kidding when he preached about sticking up for ourselves.

"When you go on a job," Knox always said, "make sure your little ass goes first class! You never know how a job's going to turn out for you. Some jobs you'll fend off drunks or ladies who want to hold you on their laps or dogs who want to knock you over and lick your face. Make sure ahead of time you've got first-class accommodations. If you don't stick up for yourself, you'll go from jobs like that back to some fleabag with the head down the hall."

Everything a dwarf needed to figure out, Knox had figured out. Even though he didn't have a hump like some of us, and was this miniature marvel of a good-looking guy, he never called himself a midget or a little person.

He'd stand on his box and shout, "The word is 'dwarf'!"

He'd lecture us that blacks didn't get anywhere calling themselves "colored" or "Negro": that all of us were duty bound to call ourselves the worst thing anyone could call us: *dwarf*—"And make it beautiful!" he'd roar.

He was the only dwarf I'd ever met whose mother and father had been dwarfs, too, though I'd heard of a few such cases. There was a dwarf who'd played in a major league baseball game who'd had dwarf parents. He was Edward Gaedel and he'd played one game for the St. Louis Browns in 1951, as a stunt. But the vast majority of us are flukes in our families.

Knox had appeared in an act with his folks in a series of second-rate carnivals, where they were billed as The Inch Family. He was also the only dwarf in Leprechaun Village who'd been earning his living since he could walk, in one form or another of sleazy show business, until both his parents died. He liked to dress all in white, and said it was because of all the years he could never wear white, when he was working carnies in dusty lots, or on the road for weeks with no place to get his clothes cleaned.

Some of them in the dorm didn't like him; some were fascinated by him; all agreed he had the smarts, and we called him "Opportunity."

There was a time in Skaneateles, New York, where I'd been sent away from a job on a cold February night because the hostess of the Valentine party hadn't been told I had a hump. She said there was no way I could play Cupid, since I was supposed to appear practically naked. Anyway, she said, Cupid wasn't a hunchback. Instead of the hundred dollars I'd been promised, in addition to a hotel room and meals, she gave me a twenty, and said to please leave before the guests arrived.

Later on in my large, comfortable room at The Skaneateles Inn, feasting on filet mignon and watching the snow fall on Skaneateles Lake, I gave silent thanks to Opportunity Knox.

I also learned, from then on, always to mention the hump, though later, as The Roach, that never mattered. I had my plastic shell covering me as I performed.

Mr. Palmer said, "Sydney, you'll *have* a room with a view, color TV, a separate bath—nothing but the best! You'll be put up at the Stardust Inn. I'm staying there myself."

Although I'd never been in La Belle, New York, I knew about the Inn. As a youngster, I'd gone with others from Twin Oaks for an outing at an amusement park on the outskirts of La Belle: Stardust Park.

"Okay," I said. "I'm glad to do it."

"Sydney," he said, getting off his desk, "La Belle has a fine library, too."

The few times we'd traveled anywhere together, I often had Mr. Palmer leave me at the local library while he took care of business.

I was comfortable in libraries, and reading was my passion.

Once, on a job, when I jumped out of a cold cherry pie at a George Washington's Birthday bachelor party, the guest of honor and I got talking.

He told me he was a psychologist, and he wanted to question me about my lifestyle. He was drunk— they always are at bachelor parties—and when he found out how much I read, he leaned into me and suggested, "You're overcompenshating, Shydney."

"For what?"

"For being sho short," he said. "You want to know sho much sho people forget your shize." Before he fell face down into his plate he added, "You esh-esh-cape that way, too."

After I became The Roach, I read even more, and then I think I was overcompensating, not for being

215

a dwarf, but for being a high school dropout.

That was something I didn't thank Opportunity Knox for; it was his example I'd followed. He used to tell us all we needed was to *say* that we'd graduated from high school. "You can fake it!" he'd say. "You can fake anything!"

Once he told me, "We can't walk to where we've got to get, Sydney, because our dear little legs won't get us there as fast as the competition's. So we've got to jump!"

In his room at the dorm in Leprechaun Village he had one of those signs that said T H I N K. T H I N K had been crossed out, and H U S T L E had been written over it. Then H U S T L E had been crossed out, and S C H E M E ! had been written over that.

Mr. Palmer shook my hand. "Sydney, then it's settled? You'll make your appearance at halftime, do the guest shot for the little La Belle girl's party, and I want you to have dinner with Mr. Hiroyuki and me one night. The rest of the time you're on your own. . . . Do you still read and watch TV at the same time?"

"Yes," I said. "That way I don't miss anything."

"From my way of looking at it, you miss two very important things," said Mr. Palmer. "You miss the point of what you're reading and the point of what you're watching."

216

He laughed and slapped my back, and we started toward the door together.

I remembered something else from my days at Leprechaun Village: a dwarf with bad legs, like mine, whom we called Artoo-Detoo, because he walked like the robot in the old film *Star Wars*.

"Imagine thinking back to a time when you were another size!" Artoo-Detoo would exclaim. "Imagine growing out of your clothes—waking up one morning and your wrists have jumped past your shirt sleeves!"

I watched myself in the wall of mirrors at the end of Mr. Palmer's office. I thought of the time I had visited Stardust Park. I was eleven then. Yet very little about my physical appearance had changed in those six years.

Three foot four and a half, still . . . the same hump, not bigger, not smaller. Legs too short for my body. My face could pass for normal. Light-blue eyes, fair teeth except for one that hung like a fang longer than the others, bucking out from the row, sandy-colored hair, good skin . . . but the rest of me was like God'd gone mad when He started making me from the neck down.

"So long, Sydney," Mr. Palmer said in the doorway. "See you in September. In La Belle."

Little Little La Belle

YOU ARE INVITED TO A PARTY

Get out your drum and fife and fiddle,
We're giving a party for Little Little,
On a September weekend here in La Belle,
Reserve a room at The Lakeside Motel,
There'll be lots to do on Sat. and Sun.
A banquet, a movie, and other fun.
It's a TADpole party for our little queen,
It's a birthday party, she'll be eighteen!
—Ava Hancock La Belle

Once when my sister, Cowboy, was little, she asked me why I wasn't "throwed away" when I was born.

"I wasn't throwed away," I told her, "because no one knew then that I was different."

"Wasn't you littler than anybody?"

"No, I wasn't."

"You was funny-looking, though, wasn't you?"

"I never looked better," I said.

That is a fact. I was a normal baby, even a big one—nine pounds and two ounces at birth. I had my mother's golden hair and my father's light-green eyes.

I don't think my sister ever stops asking herself that question, though we are thick as thieves now and united against a world that is barking mad.

Still, it has been a blight on Cowboy's life that the town dwarf is her older sister.

My mother has this thing about certain words and one of them is "pee."

She says don't say pee. I say I hate the word "urinate," it's so official-sounding for something you do with your pants down. Why do you have to use either word? she asks me. Say I have to go to the bathroom if you have to say anything, or say you'd like to wash up. My father says just say excuse me. Or just say I'll be right back.

You *could* say something fun, my father says, like I have to spend a penny, or see a man about a dog. My mother brightens at this prospect and says when *I* was in high school I said I have to use the Kitty Litter or I have to tinkle. Now they start together enthusiastically, their eyes shining with the pleasure of finding a way to avoid saying I have to pee or I have to urinate. . . . *Où est le WC?* I have to use the head. I'm going to the john. I've got to see Mrs. Jones. I have to powder my nose. I have to pay a visit to the ladies'. I have an errand. I'm going to the little girls'. I have to make wee-wee. I have to go to the loo. On and on.

Another word my mother cannot stand is "dwarf."

"Don't say 'dwarf,'" my mother says. "Call yourself a little person or a midget or a diminutive. Anything but 'dwarf.'"

That's why I prefer to call myself a dwarf.

"You picture someone with a hump when you hear the word 'dwarf,'" my mother whines at me.

I tell her, "One person's picture is another person's child. There are probably people who picture cone-headed gnomes when they hear the words 'little person' or 'midget' or 'diminutive.'"

"No, no, no, a little person or a midget or a diminutive is just a very small person, like you, Little Little, perfectly formed and perfectly beautiful."

"If I'm so perfect, what does it matter what I call myself?"

"Well, Little Little, your mouth isn't perfect."

"What's wrong with my mouth?"

"It's always open, seems to me, and there's always something sassy coming out of it."

My mother has been trying for nearly eighteen years to have a sense of humor about it. She treats Life as though it were some great force even larger than God. God gets the credit for everything good that happens, but anything bad or bewildering that happens causes her to exclaim, "Well what is Life going to do to us next!"

Giving birth to someone like me is a little like falling off a horse. The very best thing you can do is get right back on one as quickly as possible, so you lose your fear of horses. Which explains why my sister was hustled into being very soon after my mother's reeling head was just beginning to assimilate the knowledge I'd never stand taller on two feet than the family dog did on four.

Sydney Cinnamon

I was always a sentimental fellow. My eyes teared at the memories of old times and leaked at the sounds of old songs recalling past days with friends I never saw anymore. I had favorite places, too, and one of them was Stardust Park.

Immediately after I checked into The Stardust Inn that hot Friday afternoon in September, I walked down to the park, even though I knew it was closed because it was off-season.

Stardust Park was only thirty miles from The Twin Oaks Orphans' Home.

When I was at Twin Oaks, I lived in Miss Lake's cottage, where most of the handicapped lived. There were ramps for wheelchairs there instead of stairs, and sinks and closets and drinking fountains were lower to accommodate us.

All the kids who lived in Miss Lake's called it Mistakes.

There was every kind of kid to be expected there, but I was the only dwarf.

Stardust Park in the summer was a miniature Disneyland, filled with all the things you'd find in one of those places, from a 62-MPH roller coaster to a ten-foot walking chicken.

I was taken there one time with some others from Mistakes, just as the sun was rising in the early morning sky.

We always went to public places before the public was allowed in.

Some of the employees who ran the rides and sold the souvenirs were sitting around having their morning coffee.

Even though they were supposed to be prepared for the visit from Twin Oaks, they didn't look it. Their heads whirled around as we filed past them.

I always said what everyone watching us was

thinking when we came into view. OhmyGod-
doyouseewhatIsee?

There was me, and there was Wheels Potter, who
had no legs and got about on a board with roller-
skate wheels attached to it. There was Bighead
Langhorn, whose head was the size of an enormous
pumpkin set on a skinny body just a little taller
than mine. There was Wires Kaplan, with his hearing aid and his thick glasses and his bum leg. There
was Cloud, the one-armed albino, in his dark glasses
with his massive head of curly white hair the tex-
ture of steel wool. There was Pill Suchanek, whose
mother had taken some drug before Pill was born
that threw her whole body out of whack and left
her with flippers for arms. There were a few in
wheelchairs and one on crutches, all led by a
teacher we had nicknamed Robot, because his first
name was Robert and his only facial expression was
a smile, his only mood cheerful.

I paid very little attention to The Underground
City or the ten-foot chicken, the 62-MPH roller
coaster, The Space Shuttle, The Early American
Village, or Winter Wonderland.

I had gone on that expedition expressly to see
Gnomeland.

Age eleven, I had never seen another dwarf, except on television or in drawings and photographs.

When I entered Gnomeland, I could not believe my eyes. It didn't matter to me that they were all dressed in cute little costumes with bells attached to stocking caps and felt shoes on their feet, that the men wore fake white beards and some of the men and women wore cone-shaped red hats.

I laughed aloud at the buttons some wore proclaiming THERE'S NO PLACE LIKE GNOME.

I saw some with humps and some without, some wizened and ugly and some not, some old, some young—they all looked good to me.

I imagined (or I didn't) that they were all smiling at me especially, as though we all shared a fantastic secret.

Still, shyly, I stayed by Robot, who must have read my bashfulness as some sort of reluctance.

"Are you bothered by this, Sydney?"

"Bothered?"

"By this . . . commercialization?"

"I'm not bothered," I told him, not really sure what he was talking about. I added, "Anything but," longing to speak to one of them, to get my nerve up to say something.

But all I managed was a futile tug at the arm of Robot's coat when he said all right, next was the boat ride through The Underground City.

"Come on, Sydney!" Robot called as I fell

behind. "Get ready to row row row your boat!"

A hunchback dwarf with a fat cigar in his mouth stood at a microphone singing, "You're gnomebody 'til somebody loves you. . . ."

I believed that I had died and gone to heaven.

When I got back to Twin Oaks, I wrote to Gnomeland, asking how old you had to be to get a job there, and enclosed a stamped self-addressed envelope to be sure of an answer.

I remember you but stay in school, a Mr. T. Kamitses wrote back. *Get an education. Anyways, this is the last year Gnomeland will be at Stardust Park, for our contrack was not renewed. Good luck!*

I kept the letter. Even with its bad news and bad spelling it was the only communication I'd ever had with another like me.

Six years later, walking through Stardust Park, I thought about that day.

That day was the beginning of when I knew I'd make it.

Of course I knew she was Little Little La Belle the instant I saw her by the shuttered cotton candy stand.

I had a chance to look at her before she spotted me. Aside from Dora, who appeared on national television as The Dancing Lettuce Leaf in the

Melody Mayonnaise commercials, she was the most beautiful dwarf I'd ever seen.

I'd only seen Dora on the tube, watching sometimes for hours to catch a glimpse of her, so Little Little La Belle was the most beautiful dwarf I'd ever seen in person.

If I had conjured up an ideal female out of my imagination, I couldn't have surpassed what I saw standing by C O T T O N C A N D Y in the late afternoon sunlight. She had long blond hair that shined and spilled down past her shoulders, and unlike the girls at Leprechaun Village she wore a dress instead of pants. She had long legs for someone so tiny, and she was thin and still tanned from summer.

The great disadvantage of being The Roach was that, without my shell, few people knew that was who I was. Some of my groupies who waited for me regularly when I made appearances had come to know me without it, but mostly I was an anonymous dwarf.

I think I am by nature a performer, and away from the hot lights of local TV stations, or the crowds at some place like The Golden Dragon (in long lines to receive one free fortune cookie in honor of its opening), I am not pushy. I see my hump reflected in watery patterns of store windows and pull my sweater down where it rides up in back, and cover my buck fang with my hand. I have my downs.

They pass. I am normally noisy, dancing to my radio and tapes in my room over Palmer Pest Control, cracking jokes and amiable around people, and in my daydreams stepping before the footlights like Michael Dunn, who played the dwarf in the movie *Ship of Fools*. Sometimes I see myself beating a tiny tin drum like Oskar in Günter Grass's book . . . and sometimes in my act I sing under my shell, imagining myself singing windowpanes to pieces as Oskar did. I am a closet tenor who dreams of stepping out of his closet, and out from under the shell, to thrill the crowds with "Danny Boy."

When Little Little La Belle finally did look in my direction, she looked hard and directly at me, and that was when I might have nodded, waved, smiled. I froze instead. I stayed so still she might have mistaken me for one of those wooden trolls people buy at garden centers and stick on their lawns. Except I was standing in the middle of a cement sidewalk outside of the penny arcade.

I could feel my face get red, and I looked away, demonstrating at least that my head moved.

By the time I glanced up at her again, she had started walking in the opposite direction.

I followed, not at a fast pace, but I went in the

same direction she was going.

I knew she'd take a second look. We dwarfs come upon each other about as often as fish nest in trees, unless we're all working together someplace. I planned a friendly wave that I couldn't seem to bring my arms to execute, so when she sneaked a glance over her shoulder through her long golden hair, I merely trudged along in line with her, my arms paralyzed.

She walked faster. I didn't want to charge after her in hot pursuit like some dwarf rapist on the loose. I finally stood near the 62-MPH roller coaster, as stopped in my tracks as it was.

When I was at Leprechaun Village, after a day's work (we emptied ashtrays, brought pillows down poolside, paged people wanted on the telephone, ran errands, and got drinks from the bar) every night I would watch Opportunity Knox get dressed for a date. He was popular not only with other dwarfs but with normal-sized females as well. One night he slipped off for a very secret rendezvous with a guest, the wife of an Italian count, who gave him a gold signet ring inscribed *Amoretta*. That same night I had trudged along to a local movie with a group of other employees, envying his luck.

"It isn't luck, Sydney!" he'd insist. "Fate loves the fearless! Happiness hates the timid! Are you going to miss the plum because you're afraid to shake the tree? Are you always going to be the anvil, and never the hammer?"

I stood there remembering that, doing hypnosis on Little Little La Belle's back as she walked along: *You will look my way again!*

It took her around twenty seconds to register my message, to turn and take another look, and I got ready for my one little puff of a gesture. There was no small effort involved, either, with my hump, which was the reason I'd perfected the stunt years ago, so that my feet went off the ground like flying.

She gave a look and I gave back: a cartwheel.

Back on my feet, I saw she was still watching me, and with one arm across my stomach, and one behind me an inch from my hump, I bowed low.

❈ 5 ❈

Names

Me Me Me Me Me

Mark Twain claimed the difference between the right word and the almost right word was the difference between lightning and the lightning bug.

I feel that way about names.

My first book for young adults was called *Dinky Hocker Shoots Smack!* Dinky does *not* shoot smack, but she is jealous of all the time her mother spends trying to help drug addicts. While Mrs. Hocker is being honored at a community banquet for her good works, Dinky paints the four words of the book title on sidewalks and walls where no one coming from the banquet can miss them.

This is her way of dramatizing that people who don't shoot smack have problems, too.

Not a lot of adults were pleased with the title. My publisher wanted me to change it to *Inside Dinky Hocker*, since Dinky was fat, and there is a saying that inside every fat person is a thin one screaming to get out.

But I wanted a title as dramatic as Dinky, and I was disappointed when a major network presentation of the book as an *Afternoon Special* was simply called *Dinky Hocker*.

That was not Dinky's style at all: to be subtle, or cautious. She was a five-foot, four-inch, 165-pound underdog, whose sense of humor kept her afloat in the rough waters of adolescence.

Dinky was her nickname. If she had been called by her real name, Susan Hocker, she would have sounded more like the lightning bug than the lightning.

When a writer chooses names for characters, she has to believe they couldn't be called anything else. Frankenstein could never be called Anderson. Dr. Jekyll and Mr. Hyde could never be called Dr. White and Mr. Smith. Mickey Mouse wouldn't make it as Walter Mouse, and even Garfield the cat wouldn't be memorable as Mittens the cat.

I can't begin writing until I have just the right names for my characters.

I collect old high school yearbooks looking for names. I study the pictures of the kids, and read the write-ups, noticing their nicknames as well.

When I make school visits, I ask the teachers to have the kids put their names on the slips of paper with their questions to me. If I like one of their names, I ask them would they mind my using it in a book? I've never been told by one not to. More often they've begged me to give their names to one of my characters. In my Fell series there is a girl named Helen J. Keating—Keats for short. That name came as the result of one of my school visits.

Sometimes when I give writing workshops, I ask kids to think up names for 1. a tough trouble-maker; 2. a "golden boy" (good at everything and good-looking, too); 3. a "golden girl"; 4. a mean teacher; 5. a nerd; 6. a rich preppy (like Holden Caulfield from *The Catcher in the Rye*).

When I was a kid, popular names for boys were John, Tom, Bill, Henry, Bob. Girls were called Laura, Betty, Irene, and yes, Mary Jane, my own real name, which I've always hated, although my mother tried to make it more interesting by spelling it Marijane. My parents had combined their favorite names. I kept thinking, *How* could I have a mother and father with such unimaginative minds?

The old names are still around, but the new names reflect both imagination and the new ethnic mix in our country. Boys are called names like Connor, Cody, Matan, Ziv, Asa, Carlos, and Kwasi. Girls have names like Elke, Clio, Nima, Zoë, Maya, Brittany, and Fata.

For one of my books I had to come up with a name for a cockroach. This roach would turn into a little boy, so he needed an insect name as well as a human one.

I began my book: *Like all cockroaches, Shoebag was named for his place of birth.*

Shoebag's mother is called Drainboard, and his father is named Under the Toaster.

When Shoebag becomes a human, he is called Stu Bag by the family who adopt him. They add an extra *g* to the last name, and he becomes Stuart Bagg.

Shoebag became the title, as well, and I also invented a new pseudonym for myself: Mary James, from my first name, Marijane.

One of the questions kids always ask is: Why do I have so many names?

A pseudonym is your only chance to name yourself. You carry around your father's name or your husband's name, but never one you've dreamed up unless you take a pen name.

Not only is it fun to have a disguise, but it also frees you from self-consciousness. I tell kids in my workshops they can invent names for themselves, and when I read what they've written, they don't have to tell anyone they wrote it unless they want to. But the others will say what they think of what was written under their new names. Some kids who claim they have nothing to write about suddenly discover that they do—so long as no one else knows who wrote it.

Sometimes someone will come up with an ananym. That is a name spelled backward and used as a pseudonym. The TV talk show host Oprah Winfrey used an ananym of her first name for her production company—Harpo.

In this chapter from my autobiography *Me Me Me Me Me*, I am a teenager spending a summer during World War II at a lakeside cottage that my family bought, in part, to keep me out of trouble. I am home from boarding school, and our little town is filled with sailors on leave from nearby Sampson Naval Base.

Notice the slang of the day: a "slacker" was a man who managed to avoid being drafted into the service. To be "snowed" was to be deceived. We listened to music on phonograph records, which broke into little pieces if you dropped one. Notice, too, my father's male chauvinism as he discusses college with me—it's not as much a source of education as a place where I'll meet someone to marry. A girl friend from boarding school who visits me and wants to be a lawyer will be a good one, in his opinion, because "with those long legs she'll get someplace."

He wasn't very enthusiastic about my idea to be a writer, as you'll see. Still, this was the summer I chose my very first pseudonym: Eric Ranthram McKay.

from

⚜ Me Me ⚜
Me Me Me

Your Daddy Was a Sailor

The summer of 1944 I became Eric Ranthram McKay.

I think one reason for this was all the sailors pouring into our small town. There were some soldiers and marines around, too, but we knew them. They were hometown boys, coming and going from war. The sailors were another matter. On leave from nearby Sampson Naval Base, they came to us fresh from boot camp, lonely and looking for fun.

"The kind of fun a sailor is looking for might fill a few empty hours for him, but you could pay for it the rest of your life," my father said.

My mother even had a theory that "certain types" became sailors: "The wolf types are attracted to that uniform," said she.

The sailors were no small consideration when my family decided to buy a cottage on Owasco Lake, at Burtis Point (the farthest point from town), and move there for the summer.

There, at the beginning of the summer, I was marooned. My father drove into work every morning at seven, and returned at six every evening. Gas rationing made it hard for anyone to get to and from Burtis Point. There were no buses. Hitchhikers didn't fare well on the empty roads at night, which discouraged local boyfriends from visiting. "Life" was going on back in town, at the movies, at the Teen Canteen and the USO, at the kids' hangouts like Murray's.

By day I swam and sailed and looked after my kid brother, listening to my girl friends' accounts of what was happening, for hours on the telephone. By night I wrote, using my first pseudonym: Eric Ranthram McKay.

The pseudonym was chosen because my father's initials were E. R. M. After I wrote a story, I mailed it off to a magazine with a letter written on my father's stationery, engraved with his initials and our home address.

I don't know why I chose Eric, Ranthram, or McKay—I guess I just felt the name had a good ring to it.

All of Eric Ranthram McKay's stories were sad, romantic ones about the war. I subscribed to a magazine called *Writer's Digest*, which listed the needs of publications like *Good Housekeeping*, *Ladies' Home Journal*, and *Redbook*. I mailed off my stories in manila envelopes with a stamped, addressed envelope enclosed, and they came back like boomerangs, with printed rejection slips attached.

Sometimes these rejection slips had a "sorry" penciled across them, or a "try again."

Those I cherished, and saved, and used to buoy my spirits as I began new stories, and kept the old ones circulating.

At the same time Eric Ranthram McKay was writing stories, Marijane Meaker was writing servicemen—a soldier named Bob McKeon from my hometown, and a sailor named Eddie Herbold. Herbold was considered an okay sailor, since my family knew him. These "romances," by mail, were in full swing that summer.

Nights when my father arrived at the cottage with the mail, he always tried to soften the blow of a new rejection (there was often one of my self-addressed stamped envelopes in the pile) by calling out, "Herbold came through!" or "McKeon came through!" handing me one of their letters first.

Scotch-taped around my bureau mirror were pictures of Bob and Eddie, and rejection slips with a few blunt words written on them.

One story, "Your Daddy Was a Sailor," came back with the single word "Touching" written across the rejection slip.

I carried that rejection slip with me everywhere in the back pocket of my jeans.

"Your Daddy Was a Sailor" was about a girl from a small town who was warned by her parents never to date a sailor. She fell in love with one she met at a church dance. "Where did you meet this *sailor?*" her mother demanded. "I met him at church," Evelyn answered. "Reverend Lathrop introduced us." . . . Since she met him at church, she was allowed to see him. . . . But forget church; he was a sailor, wasn't he? So the inevitable happened, on a night with "stars twinkling like diamonds overhead, and the next day he would go off to fight, maybe never to return."

Skip to the future, and a woman living in a big city far from her hometown, working and raising her little boy by herself. She remembers the small town she had to leave when she became pregnant, and the quiet summer nights there, while outside her windows are the honking horns of big-city traffic. She wonders about her family, whom she hasn't seen in so long. She reads and rereads an old "last letter," a love letter from a Pacific island (suspiciously like one of Eddie Herbold's to Marijane Meaker), and then she picks up her little boy, hugs him close, and says, "Your daddy was a sailor!"

After my own father read the story, he said, "You better rewrite it and make it clear the sailor died."

"You know he died," I said. "She was rereading the last letter."

"A last letter could mean he skipped out on her. When a girl gets in trouble, more skip out than die."

In those days, when people said a girl was "in trouble," that meant only one thing: She was pregnant and unmarried.

While nobody ever described the boy as being "in trouble," he was, if he was from the same town. He usually had to marry the girl, whether he wanted to or not.

Couples who found themselves in that situation had "shotgun weddings"—so called from an old hillbilly custom in which the father of the girl would point a shotgun at the boy's head until the knot was tied.

Eric Ranthram McKay began to bother my mother.

It wasn't natural for a young girl to be closeted in a cottage bedroom night after night of a summer, writing such stories. "You need to get your mind off all that writing," my mother complained to me.

She told my father, "She doesn't want to talk with us, or play Monopoly, or listen to the radio, or do anything but stay up there by herself in her dream world, writing."

I liked being Eric Ranthram McKay, but I was restless, too.

Finally, a deal was worked out with my father. I would get a summer job in town, and he would buy me a secondhand car so I could drive back and forth to work.

In mid-July I became the owner of a 1935 LaSalle convertible, complete with rumble seat in the back (it cost him two hundred dollars), and I became employed as an operator for the telephone company.

This was a job that delighted me. Although I didn't do anything but sit in front of a switchboard, push and pull plugs, and say "Number please?" and "Thank you," I soon found out how to listen in on conversations.

Not only could I hear my girl friends gossiping, I

could hear my own mother giving out her version of our family life to friends.

I discovered that she suspected my father of having an affair with his secretary.

I discovered that she had decided to have my little brother to keep my father interested in a home-life, after my older brother and I were grown.

I also discovered that she thought I wrote so much because I was self-conscious about my long nose, that writing was my way of hiding.

Up until that moment, I hadn't thought my nose was all that long . . . and so I'd been given something to think about—obsess about—appropriate punishment, perhaps, for my snooping.

But I was back in the swing of things. I had a car, a little extra spending money (though I had to turn back some of my salary to my father, to help pay for the car), and access to the new hangout, Boysen's, as well as the old soda shop, Murray's.

Boysen's sold liquor, and even though we weren't old enough to drink, our crowd favored it because the older boys (eighteen, nineteen) and servicemen hung out there.

We went from Murray's to Boysen's, and from Boysen's to Murray's, many of the girls dragging their knitting bags with them, sitting around in these places after work knitting and drinking

Cokes, listening to the jukebox, greeting old faces in new uniforms, gossiping and watching and reading each other the latest V-mail from boyfriends.

I began dating a boy named William Dougan Annan, who was blind in one eye and couldn't get into the service because of that. He was tall and blond, really good-looking (we said "sharp"—"Oh, is he sharp!"), and we started going steady, deciding on an old song, "Where or When," as our song. This courtship we gave each other silver identification bracelets: His said *Where?*; mine said *When?*

On the day Paris was liberated, and General Eisenhower was planning his march into the French capital, I received a wire that Jan Fox, a friend from boarding school, was arriving for a visit.

"Jan Fox," I warned Dougan, "is the most sophisticated person I've ever met in my life, so we've got to fix her up with someone really sharp!"

"Jan Fox," I warned my family, "is not from small-town people, so I just hope we're not going to behave like hicks around her."

"Shall we all dress every night for dinner?" my father said.

"It's not funny," I said. "Her father's this big corporate lawyer and her mother socializes in Palm Springs, places like that."

"We're not going to act any differently than we ever act," said my mother.

"I just wish we had such a thing as a cocktail hour around here," I said.

"We have the hour," my father said, "we just don't have the cocktail."

"She drinks martinis," I said.

"Not in this house," my mother said.

"She's practically eighteen!" I said.

"I'll put a ginger ale in a cocktail glass for her at five in the afternoon," said my mother.

"With an olive," my father said.

"She also smokes," I said.

My mother said, "Not in this house."

Jan Fox arrived late on a Friday afternoon, and no matter how I tried to get my mother to change her mind about it, we had the usual Friday-night dinner, a favorite of my father's: Boston baked beans, brown bread, and salad. Choice of beverage: milk or water.

"Of course, this isn't where we really live," I explained to Jan as she unpacked up in my bedroom. "This is just a shack we bought to come to summers, to rough it. When we're up here we always eat stuff people eat at the lake, nothing fancy," I went on, just as though we didn't have baked beans fifty-two Friday nights a year. "This is sort of a health thing for us in summer, you know, lots of exercise, no smoking, no drinking."

"Don't worry about it."

"That's why I bought that tacky car, too," I said (it was my pride and joy!), "to sort of get into the spirit of things, roughing it and all . . . and it's wartime, so we don't want to be ostentatious."

"Don't worry about it."

"We'll get going later," I promised. "Dougan's fixed you up with Murray Townsend. Murray's from out of town. His people summer here, on the other side of the lake."

Then we went down to dinner, both of us in heels and leg paint, in summer dresses, ready for our dates, who were picking us up at seven thirty.

As my father dished up the beans, and passed a plate across to Jan, she said, "Beans, beans, the musical fruit, the more you eat, the more you toot!"

My father frowned while my mother blanched. Hiccuping was about the only untoward bodily function anyone in the family even admitted to, and anything that went on in the bathroom beyond bathing, shaving, or brushing your teeth was never acknowledged.

I laughed and laughed, because no one else did, and I hoped Jan Fox wouldn't notice that no one else did, while my mind whirled with disbelief that she'd said it.

Meanwhile, my mother was trying to give me the eye, to say with one long, hard look what all the vibrations from her body were already transmitting to me: the most sophisticated person you know?

After that, it wasn't so bad that my father picked up his fork and said, "Dig in," and my kid brother chewed with his mouth open.

I just figured we were all going downhill in a hand barrel, as my mother was fond of saying.

At seven thirty sharp we were still lingering at the table, over coffee, while Jan talked about her ambition to be a lawyer. Then a horn honked.

"That's them!" I said. "Let's go!"

"Sit down," said my father, as Jan and I were starting to get up.

"Our dates are here, Dad."

"Sit . . . down."

We sat down.

Another honk of the horn.

"*Dad,*" I said, "it's Murray Townsend's car. Murray's driving. He doesn't know all your rules."

The horn honked again.

We sat there.

"What's the problem?" Jan asked me.

"They have to come in and kneel before the king."

"Marijane is a lady," said my father. "When she has gentlemen callers, they come to the door, knock, wait to be invited in, enter, speak with her parents, and then leave with her, assuming that her parents find them halfway respectable."

"I love it!" Jan laughed.

"*I,*" I said, "hate it!"

By that time Dougan was knocking at the screen door.

"Come in, Dougan," my father bellowed out, "and tell the drugstore cowboy behind the wheel of the car to get himself in here, too!"

I groaned.

"I love it!" Jan kept saying.

"Tell him to bring his driver's license in with him!" my father yelled after Dougan.

I wished I was Eric Ranthram McKay, back upstairs where I belonged, writing about life instead of enduring it.

Murray Townsend, a tall, sullen blond with big white teeth, was driving his father's new, white Buick convertible, top down, radio playing full blast, as we headed into town. Jan sat beside him and bummed a cigarette from him, while Dougan and I sat in back with the wind blowing fiercely in our faces.

"I think Murray's pretty p.o.'d at your dad," Dougan told me.

"You should have warned him," I said. "It's not my fault he's that way."

"He talked to him like he was a kid. Murray's eighteen. He's going to be a doctor."

"Jan's going to be a lawyer," I said. "What do you think of her?"

Dougan shrugged. "She's all right."

"All right?" I said. "Just wait. She's sharp."

We all went to see *I'll Be Seeing You*.

Joseph Cotton played a wounded vet on furlough, who fell in love with a convicted killer, Ginger Rogers. She'd pushed her boss out of a window after he made a pass at her, and she was on Christmas leave from the penitentiary.

Jan and I both cried whenever the title tune came on the soundtrack, and at the end, but Murray said it was another silly wartime movie as we walked down to Boysen's.

I'd already warned Dougan that I wanted him to order me a real drink. In Boysen's everyone got their drinks from the bar. They rarely asked anyone at a table for proof of age, so long as the one stepping up to the bar could prove he was eighteen.

"What are you girls drinking?" Murray asked

once we were settled in a booth, and I said, "Jan likes martinis."

"Oh, I don't know," Jan said, and I said, "She drinks them until they come out of her ears."

Murray said to Dougan, "And you two?"

"Tom Collins," said Dougan.

Boysen's was packed with the usual mixture of our crowd, servicemen, sailors from Sampson, and girls from the older crowd, still in their coveralls, coming off a shift at one of the local defense plants.

The jukebox was playing songs like "I'll Walk Alone" and "Don't Get Around Much Anymore" and "Saturday Night Is the Loneliest Night in the Week."

There was a very red-cheeked, baby-faced sailor feeding it quarters, and Jan nicknamed him "Sad Eyes" a short while after she'd downed her first martini.

When she got up to help him make some selections, Murray said to me, "I thought she was supposed to be sophisticated."

"She *is*," I said.

"She doesn't even inhale," he said. "Why does she smoke if she doesn't even inhale?"

"She inhales!" I said. "*Jan?* She smokes like a chimney."

"She doesn't inhale," Dougan said.

"She drinks martinis at ten o'clock at night!" Murray said.

"What's that got to do with anything?"

Dougan said, "You drink martinis *before* dinner, not after."

"What do *you* know about martinis?" I said.

"I know what Murray told me."

"Exactly!" I said. "You're both just ganging up on her because I said she was sophisticated, and she is."

"She's got you snowed," Murray said.

"You're just teed off because she's paying attention to that cute sailor."

"I don't care who she pays attention to," Murray said. "I'm just doing Dougan a favor."

"I think she's already tipsy," Dougan said.

"On *one* martini?" I said. "She drinks them until they come out of her ears!"

"She's fried right now," said Murray.

When Jan and I went to the ladies' together, I said, "Are you all right?"

"What do you mean am I all right?"

"Nothing," I said.

"I just can't stand that hick you fixed me up with. He looks like a chipmunk."

"It's just for one night," I said.

"I like Sad Eyes better. At least he's not a slacker."

"Murray's not a slacker. He's going to be a doctor. He's going into V-Twelve."

"I like Dougan all right, but my date's a bore. It's not *your* fault."

"I tried."

"You tried," she agreed, "and thanks for trying." She pronounced it "twying" and stepped back in a sudden little lurch.

"Are you okay?"

"What's the matter with you?" she said.

We had two more rounds before we left Boysen's to make my father's one-o'clock curfew.

On the way home, we had to stop the car while she got sick.

When we got to the cottage, my father was out on the screen porch reading *A Bell for Adano* and smoking his pipe. My mother was in bed, asleep. Pale-faced and shaky, Jan went up to my room.

"Where's your friend?" my father said.

"She's dead tired," I said. "She said to say good night."

"Where did you go?"

"To the movies, to Murray's," I said. "The usual."

"That boy you fixed her up with looks like a chipmunk," said my father.

✾ ✾ ✾

The next day I discovered that Ellis Robert Meaker fascinated Jan far more than Eric Ranthram McKay did.

Instead of reading my stories, she swam out to the raft in front of our cottage with my father, and sat in the sun with him talking for hours.

"I thought that little remark of hers about musical fruit was in very poor taste," said my mother as we watched them from the lawn.

"She never says things like that," I said. "She was just recovering from the shock of being served baked beans for dinner."

"Why hasn't anyone from her family called to see that she got here all right?"

"I don't know," I said. "Ask her—no, don't," I said.

"It's very strange, a young girl traveling alone."

"Her parents are divorced," I said.

"One of them must care about what happens to her."

"Muth-*ther*," I said, "they're not small-town people. She travels all the time, probably, all over the world, probably."

"She doesn't even carry a plate to the kitchen. Did she help you make the bed this morning?"

I decided not to answer.

"I bet she didn't," my mother said.

When they finally came in from the raft, after Jan went up to change out of her bathing suit, my father said. "You could learn something from her."

"Like?"

"Like thinking about a profession for yourself, since you want to go to college."

"I'm going to be a writer."

"That's not a profession. Marijane, that's a way to starve. Now, Jan has her eye on the law as a profession. A lawyer can always make money, even a bad lawyer can make money. Writing is a nice hobby, but you can't earn a living writing. There aren't any degrees in writing."

"There are in journalism," I said.

"Journalism isn't a real profession," said my father. "I'm talking about a *profession*. Jan has a head on her shoulders. She's planning her future very carefully."

"Well, I'm glad someone in the family likes her," I said.

"She wants to be a corporate lawyer. Now that's a good choice. There're not many women in the field, and she's a looker, so she'll wrap those corporation people around her little finger."

"Like she has you," I said.

"Well, she's a nice, intelligent girl, with those long legs—she'll get someplace."

Right before my mother served lunch, the phone rang, and the caller asked for Jan.

"Well, it's about time," said my mother. "Her family *waited* long enough."

After lunch, Jan and I took a walk up the beach.

"That was Sad Eyes who called," she said. "He wants a date with me, and he's got a sailor for you."

"Are you kidding? My father'd kill me!"

"Why?"

"Because I can't date strange sailors. You just met him last night in Boysen's. How'm I going to explain that to my father?"

"Can't we say we're going somewhere by ourselves tonight?"

"We don't even know them, Jan!"

"Look, his name is Charlie Kelly. He's really nice. Can't we figure out something? Are you a prisoner of your family?"

"I suppose we can figure out something."

"We can take your car, can't we?"

"I suppose."

"It'll be fun!" she said.

. . . *The kind of fun a sailor is looking for might fill a few empty hours for him* . . . my father's baleful warning echoed in my ears, *but you could pay for it,* et cetera et cetera.

I told Dougan that Jan didn't want to go out that night, and Dougan said he wasn't surprised, she was probably still hung over.

"That means we can't go into town," I told Jan, "because Dougan will see us."

"What about your house?" Jan said. "Don't you have a key to your house?"

"The neighbors would call my mother if they saw lights on, and my car, and sailors."

"There has to be some way we could get in without them seeing the sailors. You could say you were showing me the house. I want to see it."

"What would we do there?"

"Haven't you got a phonograph, some records? We could just have a party. I don't want to drink after last night, but we could just fool around."

"What did they say they wanted to do?"

"They're from out of town. They're just these lonely guys. We'll just play records, dance—have a party!"

"Oh, I don't know," I said, but I was already figuring out that we could park my car on Marvin Avenue, go up through the fields, go in the cellar door, and have the party down there in the rec room, where there were no windows neighbors could see lights in.

I was vacillating until Jan said, "And you know

what I want to do this afternoon? I want to sit down somewhere by myself and read every one of your stories!"

She always seemed to know how to get to me.

> The Wacs and Waves are winning the war,
> Parlez-vous,
> The Wacs and Waves are winning the war,
> Parlez-vous.
> The Wacs and Waves are winning the war,
> So what the hell are we fighting for?
> Hinky, dinky, parlez-vous.

We were a motley crew.

Instead of there being two sailors, there were three: Charlie, with the baby face and sad blue eyes; Dino, with tight, black curly hair, who pronounced "bottle" "bot-ul" and was from Brooklyn, New York; Tub, who was short and very fat, perspiring and begging me for more air in our muggy, hot basement.

They brought bags of bottled beer and Cokes, pretzels and potato chips, salami and cheese and crackers.

Our rec room was decorated with World War I memorabilia, photos of my father's days in the American field corps of the French army.

The furniture was yellow wicker with bright-green cushions that smelled of mildew, and there were skis, sleds, a toboggan, bicycles, and ice skates piled around, a rolled-up dusty carpet running the length of the room, and a very old stand-up phonograph you had to crank to work. I took a flashlight up to my room, to bring down some of my records, but there wasn't much room to dance, and we got tired of winding up the machine.

We drank beer and sang and ate by candlelight, and Dino did imitations: President Roosevelt, James Cagney, Eleanor Roosevelt, Bing Crosby, on and on.

The most sophisticated person I had ever met in my entire life had turned into a blushing, giggling schoolgirl who was letting Charlie show her a new way to drink beer. He'd get a mouthful, then put his mouth against hers, open it, and let it trickle down her throat.

Dino got into a heartfelt imitation of Frank Sinatra singing "I'll Never Smile Again," and Tub was wandering around in my father's workshop, in the next room, hoping for more air, running his fingers along the edges of my father's buzz saw and saying things like "Hey, these things could take your fingers off!"

We were there for hours, long, long hours that

dragged by—I kept looking at my watch, not just because of my usual one-o'clock curfew, but because I couldn't believe sixty minutes lasted twenty-four hours; yet we were there for days, like the man who spent a year in Philadelphia one night.

My mouth really hurt from smiling smiles I didn't feel like smiling, though I couldn't let on to poor Dino that another imitation and I'd scream. Tub's white sailor suit was soaked, under his arms and all down his back, and he was beginning to smell, even from the other room.

My only consolation was that Jan Fox seemed to be having the time of her life, but that consolation was deeply depressing, and I kept thinking of the chipmunk telling me she'd had me snowed.

I know exactly the point DOOM descended.

Charlie and Jan were drinking beer from each other's mouths on the wicker couch. Tub was sitting on the rolled-up rug mopping his forehead with a large, square, white handkerchief. Dino, the Indefatigable Entertainer, was doing another imitation: ". . . This is Bob-broadcasting-to-you-from-Camp Crowder-Hope, saying—" when my father came through the basement door.

He stood there, pointing the way he'd come, barking, "OUT!"

I remember mumbling something about the boys having no way to get home and not even knowing where they were. "OUT! OUT! OUT!" he persisted, and out they went, into the night, never to be seen or heard from again.

Jan and I cleaned up after ourselves in a silence so heavy you would have had to cut it with some sharp electrical thing from the other room. My father waited, his face like a storm cloud ready to crack along with thunder and lightning.

As we headed out to his car, I managed to say, "My car's down on Marvin Avenue."

"So nearly everyone on Marvin Avenue said," he told me. "Our phone hasn't stopped ringing. You locked the door and left your lights on!"

Then he said, "The motor's probably dead anyway. We'll stop and turn off the lights, and you can get it tomorrow when—"

"We didn't mean anything wrong, Mr. Meaker." Jan tried to calm him down.

"Tomorrow," my father continued, "when we're on the way to the train Jan is catching."

We drove back to Burtis Point in silence, except for the sound of hiccups from Jan Fox and one solitary, under-the-breath remark from my father: "Sailors!"

❈ ❈ ❈

I corresponded with Jan Fox for a while, and then lost track of her.

Before I went away to boarding school, I always thought I was a rich kid. I always thought my family was really sophisticated.

Jan Fox, and the boarding-school experience, got me thinking twice about this, and for the first time I began to meet kids who made me feel like the small-town girl I really was.

I went through a period during which I decided my family were really these awful hicks, nothing but an embarrassment to me. Why did my mother wear so much junk jewelry? Why did my father have to say things like "Soup's on!" instead of "Dinner's ready," or "How do?" instead of "How do you do?" Why did my mother have to mention the price of everything, and talk about "bargains"? Why didn't we ever have wine with dinner, or go to concerts, and why did my father have to call classical music "long-hair noise"?

Why didn't we collect art, ride horseback, have dinner parties, or serve cocktails?

I was very thankful I hadn't chosen a boarding school close to home, and that the war made it impossible for them to visit, because I was sure my family would just be a humiliation to me.

My family was probably wondering around the same time what they'd done wrong to produce this girl who called herself Eric Ranthram McKay.

Once I received a letter from a kid doing a paper on M. E. Kerr.

"Why did you decide to name your pen?" he asked me.

I don't think my father's E. R. M. stationery was the sole reason I began writing under a pen name. I think I was drawn to the idea I could create this separate identity for myself, and write about people I knew without them ever knowing who was telling their secrets.

Since nearly all of my pseudonyms were male, I must have also felt that a female wouldn't be taken seriously.

Even when I finally talked my father into letting me go to journalism school, he argued that no matter whether or not the University of Missouri had a better school than the one in nearby Syracuse, New York, I should go to Syracuse.

"Why?" I asked him.

"Because if you go to Missouri," he said, "you'll marry a boy from Missouri. You'll live in Missouri. You'll never get back for holidays, and we'll see very little of you."

From his viewpoint, it wasn't what a girl studied, it was where. All college did was provide a place for you to meet your future husband.

Once, I toyed with the idea of becoming a librarian, since I loved libraries so much. I could work in a library and write on the side.

"That's a terrible idea," my father said. "If you go to library school, you'll never meet a man!"

Years and years later, I discovered I wasn't the only one

who felt a female wouldn't be taken seriously. When I first began writing suspense stories for Fawcett Publications, my editor suggested that I take a male pseudonym.

"You tell a fast, tough story," he said, "and you'll lose your credibility with a name like Marijane Meaker."

I chose the pen name Vin Packer, after talking about the problem over dinner with one friend whose first name was Vin and another whose last name was Packer.

Even in the '60's, when I did a nonfiction book on suicide for Doubleday, called Sudden Endings, my editor suggested that I call myself M. J. Meaker, instead of Marijane Meaker.

"Marijane," she said, "isn't right for a book on suicide."

While I did do a few novels under my real name, I always felt better when I "named my pen."

When I named it M. E. Kerr, it was a play on my last name, and probably a hangover from the days when I felt, along with others, that a female writer wouldn't sell as well as a male would.

I feel a great deal of satisfaction being her.

Kids write and tell you what they think.

"When I see your name on the cover of books," a kid wrote me once, "I know that half the time they're good."

Another kid wrote saying, "Dear M. E. Kerr, we were forced to read you in English class."

What more could a writer ask for than a captive audience?

ABOUT THE AUTHOR

M. E. Kerr, winner of the Margaret A. Edwards Award for her lifetime achievement in writing for young adults, is the author of nineteen highly acclaimed books. She lives in East Hampton, NY, where she leads the famous Ashawagh Hall Writers' Workshop.